What Peo
Diane Albano ~... ... ... ~ ~... ... .

"*The Art of Being Nice* offers moving stories about the pitfalls of 'being nice' and practical strategies for more empowered living. In this book, you're invited to break free from old patterns and create new behaviors that will inevitably lead to greater fulfillment in life."

— Marci Shimoff,
#1 New York Times Bestselling Author of *Happy for No Reason* and *Chicken Soup for the Woman's Soul*

"Once in a great while, there comes a book that opens the door for those of us who have silenced ourselves and allowed ourselves to be shut down; the day we read that book, we realize we can no longer be compromised in order to be accepted. Diane Albano's *The Art of Being Nice* demonstrates how to be heard, and it gives you, through self-discovery exercises, a voice to be respected and appreciated. This book is must buy for those individuals who now desire to be understood and acknowledged!"

— Dr. Michael Gross,
Author of *The Spiritual Primer: Reconnecting to God to Experience Your True Source's Love, Joy and Happiness*

"Have you ever considered how 'being nice' might actually be getting in your way? In *The Art of Being Nice*, Dr. Albano skillfully helps the reader reflect on this powerful conditioned response using real life lessons, insightful questions, and practical strategies. It's a must-read for anyone who thinks that 'nice' is a voice!"

— Dr. Connie Hebert,
National Literacy Consultant, and Author of
The Teachable Minute: The Secret to Raising Smart & Appreciative Kids

"Dr. Diane Albano is a talented, highly skilled, certified professional leadership consultant and life coach. Her experience as a parent, teacher, administrator, professional speaker, and exceptional coach helps Diane's clients create the results they desire in their workplaces and personal lives. Diane's heartfelt passion, energy, unique knowledge, and training can support and empower you to create a life you truly love living!"

— Jennifer Jimmenez,
Founder of Vibrant Healthy Woman, Transformation Coach and Health and Well-Being Expert

"In *The Art of Being Nice*, Diane Albano recalls her struggle to overcome her fear of upsetting people by not always pleasing them. It's a difficult road to walk, so she is now sharing her story and surefire methods for everyone else who wants to live a more balanced life as a kind person who still can speak up for themselves."

— Patrick Snow,
Publishing Coachand International Best-Selling Author
of *Creating Your Own Destiny* and *Boy Entrepreneur*

"We all want to be nice, but when people take advantage of that, we need to be ready to set boundaries that protect our wellbeing and interests. Being nice, as Diane Albano shows in this book, definitely is an art. Once you read this book and put to work her hard-earned advice, you'll feel like Picasso, a master artist at navigating between social mores and getting what you want."

— Tyler R. Tichelaar,
PhD and Award-Winning Author of
Narrow Lives and *The Best Place*

"While I came to Diane seeking career guidance, what I received was so much more. Diane comes to coaching from a spiritual and holistic perspective. So rather than just dealing with one discrete issue, our work was much broader. We talked about underlying issues, exploring gratitude, manifesting a vision of the future, and listening to the small voice. With Diane's help and encouragement, I'm about to embark on a new adventure that will take me out of my rut and allow me to explore some exciting new possibilities."

— Daniel B.,
Non-Profit Administrator, New York

"Diane has supported me for more than ten years in a variety of areas, including leadership development, team building, parenting, and increasing my personal power. In all instances, she has skillfully used goal setting, inquiry, and reflection to assist me in achieving my goals. All the while, she carefully designed our work together in affirmations, honest feedback, and wise instruction. Diane's personal commitment to her craft, her students, clients, and friends is a gift she generously pours without expectation of personal gain."

— N. Eschler,
Educational Leader

"Diane helped me focus my thoughts on what I valued and still desired in terms of personal growth and achievement. It gave me permission to even think about achieving. After all, wasn't I now retired? Diane helped me articulate what I still desired in my life. She helped me speak my dreams and then helped me shape them into a plan of action."

— Gloria Jean,
Educational Consultant

"Working with Diane is such a gift. She listens with such loving presence, then she organizes what I've shared and reflects it back to me, with uncanny wisdom and clarity. I don't need to understand and present my challenges; I need only to talk about them (blurt them out!). Diane does the heavy lifting. She has a way of lifting me up, dusting me off, and pointing me in the right direction. She addresses tough subjects with non-judgment, warmth, and humor. I feel great after each conversation we have."

— Linda Watkins,
Energy Kinesiologist,
YourStellarHealth.com

"Diane is a warm, friendly, genuinely caring person who has the ability to draw out the best in you, to help you see your strengths. Then she helps you go forward into the world to pursue your dreams and goals with that mindset of self-worth and confidence. She helps you set concrete action steps to move toward your ultimate dream-life."

— Carol Marguiles,
Musician

The Art of
Being
Nice

Own Your Voice for
Greater Power and Fulfillment

AVIVA
PUBLISHING
New York

Diane Albano, Ed.D.

Kate,
Believe Dreams!
in your
With gratitude
and love,
Diane

**With gratitude and love
to my loving parents,
Earl and Lillian, grandmother
Marion, and son, Ian.**

Contents

Introduction

Are you one of the many individuals in this world who have learned how to be nice? I am not talking about being kind or polite, but developing from an early age the internalized behavior of being nice, often to a fault. That was me.

This book is written from my life experiences as well as those of others who have shared their life stories with me. We all experienced the imprinted message of "being nice" as children and the power, pitfalls, and impact it had upon us into adulthood. I've written this book for women and men who can identify with life patterns of compromising their truth, their God-given talent and abilities, and minimizing the power of owning their voices for greater freedom and fulfillment.

Being nice became such a habit that I withheld speaking my truth in order to keep the peace. I didn't want to rock the boat or hurt others' feelings. I sought approval and wanted to be loved. I was so attached to this way of being that I let it deeply define me, and in the process, I lost the true essence of who I *am*.

Can you identify with playing small in the world or shrinking so others won't feel insecure? What is it costing you in your life? It was costing me my health, my happiness, and my relationships at home and at work. It felt safer to mask my true feelings and thoughts. As an adult, I learned these patterns of behavior no longer served my conscious or unconscious mind. I acquired a sense of freedom and joy knowing I no longer needed to compromise my own needs and desires to please others or seek approval and love.

I had to learn to change, and I am grateful now that I am integrating the tools of transformation for a happier, freer, and more fulfilling life. I learned to embrace my journey. I decided to write this book to share my life experiences with others so they will know they are not alone. My intention is to provide you with an opportunity to open your heart as a divine being and to reflect on what may be stopping you from owning your greatness.

As a professional life coach, I work with individuals and groups across the country to gain insight and to identify what actions will support them in having a sense of clarity, purpose, freedom, confidence, and courage. Everyone deserves to be heard, to be respected, and to know they are more than enough.

Writing this book has been an amazing journey of self-discovery, healing, and transformation. I want that for you as well. What has "being nice" and keeping quiet cost you in your life? Do you hold resentments, but dare not say what is really in your heart? Are you afraid to lose love and attention? Might you lose your job? Will your speaking up in your family make waves? By changing how you think about and approach life, I guarantee that you will open yourself to greater confidence, satisfaction, and love. The love of yourself.

When I think about my journey, the song "Amazing Grace" comes to my mind. I related to the words of feeling lost because I was truly lost, hardly aware! I was trying so hard to be the good girl by staying in control, pleasing others to get love and attention, and trying to make others happy. I was compromising my own happiness, freedom, worthiness, and self-love. I am pleased to say I have been able to let go of the grip many of my stories had on me even into adulthood. The good news is you, too, can transform your personal story of struggle, betrayal, and isolation to achieve greater fulfillment, happiness, freedom, and love.

HOW TO USE THIS BOOK

You are invited to use this book as a personal journal to reflect your own path. *The Art of Being Nice* offers an opportunity for reflection by providing evocative questions in the Exercise section at the end of each chapter with spaces to write down your responses.

A Strategies section is included in each chapter to provide you with additional ideas and suggestions to help you change your behavior as you become a more empowered, confident, and courageous individual.

If you are reluctant or more comfortable not writing in the spaces provided, please purchase a special notebook to journal your thoughts and responses to the questions throughout the chapters. This is your process. Make it work for you!

Are you ready now to begin your journey? Are you ready to quit holding back who you are, so you can be true to yourself and still live a courageous, satisfying, and fulfilling life? I know you are. Let's go on this journey.

Diane Albano

Chapter 1

Feeling Heard and Nurtured

"And no one will listen to us until we listen to ourselves."
— Marianne Williamson

Have you ever felt you were not being heard or nurtured? As babies, we cried and our parents and guardians responded by feeding us, changing us, and giving us attention and love. For most of us, our basic needs were met. Yet somewhere between those years and this moment, we silenced ourselves as we were taught how to show up in this world.

I was taught to be *nice.*

At the 2018 Golden Globe Awards, Oprah Winfrey was the recipient of the Cecil B. DeMille Award for lifetime achievement. Her acceptance speech was dynamic, passionately delivered, and designed to speak particularly to young girls, women, and the men who support them. She proclaimed, "For too long women have not been heard or believed. It is time to speak your truth!" I admire Oprah's commitment to help women find their voices, heal their lives, and empower other women. Oprah has been willing to give her voice to address the struggles, abuse, lies about, and mistreatment of women.

Have you ever felt it is safer to be invisible? Often as a child, I was told my feelings or perceptions were not accurate, which created a foundation for me of doubting and questioning my reality and myself. Life's challenges are labeled by the belief systems of all the adults who interact in a child's life. These messages are communicated over and over to that child as they grow and develop.

We all have stories to tell. Hopefully, by sharing some of my and others' experiences, you will feel less alone in finding your voice to achieve greater happiness, fulfillment, and freedom.

A LIFELONG PROCESS

One of my greatest insights in learning to speak my truth is that this is a lifelong process! Let me begin by telling you about my upbringing. My mother was raised in an Irish Catholic family of eight children living in a two-family house at the top of the hill from the well-known Mission Church in Boston. She would tell me stories about walking with her siblings every day to morning Mass and to school at the bottom of the hill, then walking home for lunch and returning to school. Years later, she met my dad at a dance. During World War II, my father enlisted in the Army and was sent to the Philippines as a paratrooper. My mom would tell me stories of their continued love affair via letters with hearts written on the envelopes. Shortly after my dad fulfilled his tour of duty and returned to the States, they were married in the same church my mom knew and loved. For a time, they lived close to all of her family. My mother longed for a big family just like she had growing up. As the years passed, she became anxious and saddened to see all of her sisters starting their own families while she still didn't have children.

Seven years later, my parents found out they were finally having a baby. They were ecstatic. After I was born, with only my dad's income and my mom leaving her job to be home with a new baby, they could not afford the monthly expenses of the house where they had been living. A traumatic transition followed for my mother when they moved away from her large family nucleus to a more affordable, small rural area about twenty-five miles west of Boston and closer to where my dad's mother lived.

This relocation created a sense of both financial and emotional loss for my mother. She was very lonely and missed her mother, brothers, and sisters, all of whom still lived in Boston. My dad was responsible for being the family breadwinner; he took on extra jobs and worked the night shift. Being an only child, my nighttime routines were not like those of most children who went to bed early. My mother kept me up to keep her company. Maybe that is why, to this day, I refer to myself as a night owl.

For my mother, this period became one of isolation and depression. She had never learned to drive and she hadn't made friends where we now lived. I was the center of her world. She occupied part of her time by talking daily on the phone with her different sisters.

We lived in an area without any children in the immediate neighborhood. I yearned for playmates. My mother would always take an afternoon nap and lock the screen door, telling me not to go outside and to be nice and quiet like a good girl. Sometimes, we would play board games when she got up. I remember being creative by drawing, coloring, and playing with my dolls; I even created an imaginary friend who would play with and listen to me. I was at a critical stage in my development, one during which children formulate their sense of security, self-worth, and confidence. I was learning at an early age that in order to get attention, I needed to be a nice girl and comply. Upon reflection, I see this period also provided me with an opportunity to develop my creativity, imagination, and self-motivation.

As I got older, I became more aware of my mother self-medicating with alcohol, which led her into a greater depression. Today, after years of personal growth, I understand she was doing her best with what she knew. While I was growing up, her love didn't always feel nurturing; it felt controlling of my every action. For instance, as a teenager, in the days before cellphones, I usually could not talk on the phone without her listening in on the extension.

RELATING

At the end of one of my Vision Workshops, a woman came up to me to share her story of when she was a little girl. Beth described herself as a child with sparkling eyes who loved reading and asking questions with joy and wonder. Beth had three siblings, and as the oldest, she often questioned her mother's decisions for herself or her sisters. However, when she spoke her truth, she was often reprimanded and scolded. Her mother literally washed out her mouth with soap, and she often followed it up by placing pepper on her tongue. It did not take long for this young girl and her sisters to learn that speaking up or challenging anyone's beliefs was not a safe thing to do.

I find it fascinating that at such an early age, we intuitively choose coping mechanisms to respond to our environment. Evidence-based research, articles, books, and the best self-help gurus tell us our thoughts have a direct impact on our health, wellness, and relationships. Negative thoughts perpetuate more negativity, discouragement, and depressed thinking. Positive thoughts bring about more joy, abundance, and happiness. It has taken me decades of reading, research, and therapy to support myself in using my voice to be heard.

In her book *Women's Bodies, Women's Wisdom*, Dr. Christiane Northrup writes how as a medical doctor and gynecologist, her Western medicine training did not teach her to focus or listen to the patient's deep knowing and heal from the inside, but instead, to heal and treat from the outside. Today, Northrup honors women's voices, intuition, thoughts, and actions, and how they impact their health. These suggestions offered me a new way of thinking about myself.

I have always been curious to learn more about the power of the conscious and subconscious minds, hypnosis, self-improvement, and so on. Yet I was always coming from a place of feeling something was missing. I needed to fix me, and I believed someone else knew better than I did. My self-confidence and emotional development were lagging in my own thinking. Thoughts that would drive my happiness, peace, and joy felt beyond what was possible in nurturing myself.

For many years, I lived my life as a martyr, as if life were happening "to me." I learned to cover up all my uncertainty, fear, and doubt by trying to appear perfect. I was trying to seek approval and love. This survival strategy became ingrained in my life's story, but it was not a healthy one. What I have learned is that how we nurture ourselves is directly related to our experiences, and we all have the ability to live our lives differently if we choose. Sometimes, living differently involves communicating clearly our desires and wants; other times, it requires us to set boundaries, establish routines, and intentionally design food and spending plans, all to support us in taking care of ourselves.

I am grateful to all those individuals who have coached and counseled me through my adult years. However, ultimately, I realized I was responsible for being the main character in my game of life and being willing to change my beliefs that no longer served me.

EXERCISE

Where in your life have you felt you have not been heard?

_____

_____

_____

_____

_____

Where and when have you silenced your truth?

_____

_____

_____

_____

_____

Next time, what might be one step you can take to speak up?

_____

_____

_____

_____

_____

STRATEGIES: FEELING HEARD AND NURTURED

- Take a deep breath before having any reactions with a family member or coworker. Ask yourself: What is the most loving response I can make in this moment?

- Use "I" statements to share how you are feeling or to repeat a request.

- Understand that you deserve to be heard in all of your relationships both at work and at home.

- Remember it is not always what you say but how you say it!

- Nurture yourself. Get plenty of exercise. Eat more veggies, fruits, and protein. Get plenty of rest and drink more water.

- Buy some flowers on the way home for your table.

- Go for a walk in nature.

SUMMARY

All of us have experienced some version of not being heard as a child and as an adult. Are we listening better to ourselves now and to our children more attentively? If asked, would more children say their parents or teachers are hearing them? Are we really listening to children with an open heart that is full of joy, love, and full acceptance?

When we engage in life by operating out of our old beliefs, we are hindering our listening to our own inner voices so that we repeat patterns that are familiar, comfortable, and often not helpful.

We have the ability and power to give to ourselves what as children we looked to someone else to give us. It is called self-love. Reading those words may elicit feelings of support, caring, and empowerment for our own growth and development and that of others. It may sound clichéd, but what we do know is that people who have greater freedom and happiness have learned to listen to themselves without judgment of themselves or others.

It's your time to wake up, be present to all that life has to offer, and be open and willing to listen and nurture yourself first.

Chapter 2

Taking Yourself Everywhere

"You are responsible for your life. You can't keep blaming somebody else for your dysfunction. Life is really about moving on."
— Oprah Winfrey

We are responsible for our thoughts, actions, and outcomes. Learning about ourselves and then changing how we perceive the world requires great faith and commitment. No matter how old you are, you can have a breakthrough at any time in your life. My clients have had amazing results once they realized they could manifest opportunities and live a life that is greater than their circumstances. I hope through reading this book you will come to believe the same and make it your new reality.

BEYOND THE JOB

My client Sarah was a middle-level supervisor who had worked for the State for more than twenty-five years. She had spent most of her life as a hardworking and loyal employee. She loved her relationships with the people she supervised, and she enjoyed seeing them grow and develop as individuals and as a team. However, Sarah knew she wanted to feel more fulfilled and joyful. While she got occasional glimpses of such a life, she had a hard time fully envisioning what it would look like.

Sarah's children were now grown and lived in two different parts of the country; they did not communicate regularly with her because of their busy schedules and lives. Sarah was now single, and her friendships were primarily with a few coworkers. Sarah would have dinners out, go to movies, and talk about work. Periodically, she would travel to visit her adult children. Sarah now realized she had been looking outside of herself to her children and coworkers to make her feel happy and needed.

Then things began to change for Sarah at work. New upper management had a different leadership style; they seemed to place less value on relationship building and more on bottom-line production. Sarah's job had become her identity, but with the changes at work, she was feeling less satisfied and happy.

Since her job paid well and had good benefits,

Sarah stayed with the company a few more years, all the while feeling more and more stuck and depressed. She realized all of her time and energy had been going into her job, and she had little time or energy to bring other fun things into her life.

One evening, Sarah attended a workshop for empty-nesters. It was designed for the attendees to explore and envision what they would be doing three years from now. This workshop provided an opportunity for Sarah to think about and change some of her perceptions. She identified some action steps to create a more fulfilling life and think about what brought her joy. She loved floral arranging, but she had not even thought about it for more than twenty years. Later, Sarah told me she was focusing on what made her happy. She had decluttered an extra bedroom that had become a junk room and had signed up for a continuing education class on floral arrangement.

CAN YOU RELATE?

Have you ever experienced feeling like all you do is work?

My desire when I began studying personal development was to have a greater understanding of myself and how my actions were impacting my health, wellbeing, and happiness. When I felt like a victim or martyr, I would just try harder to take care of others. Perfectionism was a trait I learned well, and it did serve my grades, keeping things organized, and looking good. However, it was a taking a toll on me and others. It took years for me to unravel the impact of my need for perfectionism. It was not yet obvious to me that I was abdicating my responsibility to take care of my own mind, body, and spirit. In fact, I would have felt insulted if anyone ever considered I was not being responsible in any way—even to myself.

BEING NICE AND IN CONTROL

One aha moment I had was that being nice was a way for me to be in control. All of a sudden, being nice was not as endearing a quality. I realized I would step up and take control to get things done when I felt others were failing to do their own jobs or be responsible. I would get annoyed and frustrated at the lack of others' participation and take charge.

My frustration with others often drove how I interacted at home and at work. You might identify with some of my thoughts in this situation: "If only they would be different, then I would be happy," "Look at what I have done for you," "What about me?"

These are only a few examples of the unproductive conversations and thoughts that ticker-taped through my mind. I was later delighted to know I was not alone when I spoke with hundreds of women and men who shared similar stories of feeling this way while I was writing this book. Often, we rely too much on our personal relationships and activities at home and work to bring us joy, love, and fulfillment. For many of us, myself included, we were raised this way. Keeping Mom, Dad, our grandparents, teachers, etc. happy was how we felt safe and loved. The payoff of being nice provided a feeling of being in control, and it gave us recognition and praise.

TAKING YOURSELF EVERYWHERE

Keep in mind that we take ourselves everywhere. Personally, I needed to accept responsibility for my thoughts and the choices I made at home and work. I thought I was being one way at home and another way at work, compartmentalizing the two, but I did not realize how doing so was impacting my happiness. My belief was that things were happening to me, so at times, I felt like a victim. My thoughts were not empowering me. Instead, when things went wrong, I found myself asking, "Why is this happening to me?" I believed others could have fulfilling relationships, but that wasn't in the cards for me.

One day, some issues arose with my supervisor, so I went to the Employee Assistance Program. The program was designed to offer short-term counseling support to help employees process a situation and seek a solution. It guaranteed confidentiality and anonymity. I remember thinking, *I hope no one finds out*. I found it was a safe place to disclose my feelings and frustrations and to be heard. I remember telling the counselor, "At work, I am one way, but I am different at home." I was encouraged to begin questioning this dichotomy of thought. Was it really true?

ON AUTOPILOT

For years, my thinking focused more on my job and position. They defined who I was—they became my identity. I was trying to make a difference and support others. I was staying busy day after day and always had a to-do list. I was often bringing work home and trying to finish it after my son was asleep. And the hamster's wheel spun. I call this lifestyle being on autopilot. I was truly caught in the trap. It was very easy not to look at the bigger picture.

Have you or anyone you've known ever said, "This is just the way I am"? How do you respond to that statement? In many of my coaching sessions, I hear clients refer to family members or a life partner using those words to them. What then is our role in this interaction? Do we accept and try to take responsibility to fix a situation, be the caretaker, try to make it better, or tolerate it and not speak up?

It took me a long time to understand the dynamics of the role I played in all of my relationships. Of course, I was always coming from a place of trying to be nice, seeking approval, and wanting to look good so people wouldn't see that deep down inside I might feel angry or disappointed. Being nice resulted in not feeling happy or at peace with myself.

EVOLVING

It has taken me decades to unravel my personal journey of people pleasing while navigating through uncertainly and dodging life's landmines. I often think about the expressions, "We learn the most through our mistakes," "Often the darkness is needed before we see the light" and "There's a light at the end of the tunnel." I struggled to shift my thinking from minimizing my needs and beliefs so I would feel safe, and instead, accept that it was okay to be vulnerable and let others know I didn't have all the answers.

Marci Shimoff and Dr. Sue Morter, well-known leaders in Your Year of Miracles groups, make a distinction between our need to be perfect versus perfectionism. They say we are already perfect, whole, and complete. Perfectionism is a self-destructive belief system that comes from within us and causes us to compensate or diminish ourselves. It is a matter of perception. In her book *Gifts of Imperfection: Let Go of Who You Think You're Supposed to Be* and *Embrace Who You Are*, Brené Brown speaks to how our shame, judgment, and blame contribute to these self-destructive thoughts, leading us to minimize ourselves.

Most people knew me in my different roles and responsibilities of mom, daughter, wife, sister, friend, significant other, teacher, and administrator. I was outwardly successful on many fronts, but increasingly discontent on the inside.

One of my greatest lessons was to step back to listen to my own thoughts and feelings and to act based on what is best for me. Rather than do things to please someone else, I needed to be honest and please me first. I learned this is not a selfish act. Today, I take better care of myself, and I no longer need to compartmentalize, separating myself in situations in my life to accommodate my surroundings. I've learned I cannot control how someone reacts; nor can I take away their pain.

I once worked with a wonderful, caring school superintendent. He always had words of wisdom and shared his joy and passion about lifelong learning. He told me it really doesn't matter how old you are; so long as you love learning, you will continue to grow and develop. I am so grateful for his wisdom.

EXERCISE

How has separating yourself or compartmentalizing your personal and work lives affected your personal happiness? How have the stresses of your job impacted your personal life?

_____

_____

_____

_____

_____

What holds you back from speaking your truth in your personal relationships or on the job? How is being held back impacting your health and wellness?

_____

_____

_____

_____

_____

What is one step you can take to have less perfectionistic thoughts?

_____

_____

_____

_____

_____

STRATEGIES: TAKING YOURSELF EVERYWHERE

- Notice what you are noticing. Ask yourself questions: Are you selling yourself short? Are you angry? Are you acquiescing to someone else?

- Be clear: What are you wanting? Don't expect others to know what you want. This is particularly important to remember at home with your family and friends.

- Program your phone with a positive message for the day as a reminder to you of the special and talented person you are.

- Use a personal journal to jot down your thoughts and feelings. Notice how your patterns of behavior create more happiness or discontent. What action might you take to bring yourself greater fulfillment?

SUMMARY

Our life journey is a process, not a destination. Today, there are times when I still become silent because I'm afraid of how to say something without hurting another's feelings. These behaviors are old patterns of thinking and behaving. Repatterning responses and behaviors takes time.

We all have a shadow side composed of the secrets and untruths we use to protect ourselves, to feel safe, to be accepted, or to fit in. Only when we become aware of how we communicate with others does it open the door to acting and interacting differently in all our relationships.

How we say and do things is a choice and in our control. Hence, gently responding or asking to revisit something if you can't say something in the moment is very powerful for personal growth. Ultimately, we take ourselves everywhere.

No matter how much we wish others' behaviors would change, in the end, we can only change ourselves.

Chapter 3

Listening to the Small Voice Within

"Have the courage to follow your heart and intuition."
— Steve Jobs

Steve Jobs, known for his innovative contributions to Apple Inc., reminded us, "Your time is limited, so don't waste it living someone else's life. Don't let the noise of others' opinions drown out your own inner voice." Are you living your life this way?

My friends and family often used to see me as one of those self-help junkies. How many new programs might I buy and/or participate in? One friend said to me, "Why are you always looking for something? Can't you just be happy with who you are and what you have?" Was I doing that? I always had a deep desire to help others, but this time it was my turn to have a greater understanding of who I was and achieve a greater sense of freedom and inner fulfillment. My son was now a teenager and off with his own friends. Up until then, I had been a dutiful daughter, wife, mom, and friend—much of the time, being nice with a price. I knew there was more. My soul yearned for a more vibrant, healthy, and prosperous lifestyle.

In truth, I had spent several more years looking for external, heartfelt, loving relationships to fill an inner void that felt so deep. Frequently, I second-guessed what I really wanted, and I was always trying to figure things out and analyze everyone and everything. It was exhausting.

I was letting the chatter in my mind drive a lot of decision-making, and it motivated me to work longer hours, care for others before myself, and thereby fulfill a need to be needed, loved, and successful. My life felt like I was like riding a roller coaster from one crisis or drama to isolation and loneliness. My patterns of behavior sowed what I was experiencing. Referencing Steve Jobs' quote, I now needed to demonstrate the courage necessary to follow my heart and intuition.

CONSCIOUSLY CHOOSING

At that time, I was not consciously taking responsibility for my own choices that kept me stuck and discontent. Today, I realize the small voice within me was always there; I just was not listening to it or trusting that I could give myself permission to make a different choice.

Why do we feel we need permission to act on things that are really ours to decide?

If you've ever experienced such feelings, be gentle with yourself. It took me years of support and coaching to reach this point in my journey!

Many years ago, I broke off a relationship with a man by telling him he just wasn't spiritual enough. Really? As my grandmother would say, that was "The pot calling the kettle black"! My voice within was really speaking to me when I used those words. It was not about him at all; it was really about me. It took me a while to appreciate that he had come into my life for a purpose—so I would realize my own need to become more spiritual.

As I began to listen more to my heart and inner voice, I became filled with greater faith. I realized I deserved more, and I was not going to settle for things that did not align with my greater good. I wanted a greater connection with my Divine Source, my Spirit, which I choose to call God. By surrendering the thoughts that weren't serving me, I felt less alone, more content, and at peace.

A DAY OFF

Marie had been looking forward to taking a mental health day off from work for three weeks. She had plans to clean and organize her apartment, go for a walk in the beautiful park down the street that she never made time to experience, and meet some friends for supper. Sleeping in for her was the first luxury of the day.

As Marie made her morning coffee and sat by the window overlooking the park, she immediately started reading her work email, followed by several texts. Ugh—she had just dipped more than her toe into work. Marie could feel her anxiety and anger begin to creep into her planned day of freedom and relaxation. The email from her boss read: *I will not be in the office next week; I need your report by noon tomorrow.* Marie knew her boss was going on vacation, and he always wanted to review all reports before they went to the board members.

Staring at the email, she told herself she should have finished the report before she left, but she had made a conscious decision to finish the report after her day off. Annoyed at the request, but really more annoyed with herself, Marie started to attend to some of the things she needed to do in her apartment. However, completing the report was gnawing at her and consuming her thoughts. Marie felt less peaceful throughout her day. She decided to have an earlier dinner with her friends so she could come home to work on the report. However, as the day progressed, Marie let the report drift out of her mind; getting home late, she set the alarm early, intending to go into work early to meet her deadline. She realized that procrastinating had created more stress and less peace of mind for her.

VOICE WITHIN

How many of us relate to the little voice within that says, "I should have acted"? When we procrastinate, it is often a result of wanting something to be perfect. We become anxious and fearful, which keeps us from focusing on just getting the job done.

A few years ago, I attended Dream Builder Live Workshops and the Life Mastery Program at the Life Mastery Institute to become a Dream Builder Coach and a Certified Life Mastery Consultant. One of the people I had the privilege to work with at the Life Mastery Institute was its founder, Mary Morrissey. Mary has been an international speaker, best-selling author, consultant, visionary, and empowerment specialist for more than forty years. Mary often refers to the small voice within as our intuition, one of the six laws of the Universe. Our intuition is our inner guidance that calls to us, but we often ignore.

Mary provides a simple example of intuition: It's

a bright sunny day; as you walk out the door, you think, *Maybe I should bring my umbrella*. Of course, your conscious self says, *That's ridiculous*, and you leave it hanging by the door. Later in the afternoon, when the dark rain cloud comes your way, you briefly remember that something told you to take an umbrella, but you didn't.

How many times have you been thinking about someone, and then the phone rings and it's them? These are all little signs of tuning into our inner knowing.

One summer evening while driving home from visiting a friend, I was in a car accident. I was hit right behind the driver's seat by a pickup truck going through a red light. It all happened so quickly that I found myself just praying to be divinely protected, and as my car was in a spin, I heard a voice say, "Put your foot on the brake." Miraculously, I was still conscious, but with significant bruising, neck, and back pain. My car was totaled. I had loved my car; it had served me well and was paid off! Although I was given a rental, all the doctors' appointments, insurance calls, and search for another vehicle felt overwhelming.

Days later, I purchased another car with low mileage and a good reputation for being durable and safe. Like many of us with a new vehicle, I was extra-careful when driving and I parked the car away from others. That weekend, I drove to my niece's baby shower in Massachusetts. It was the first time I had driven any distance since my accident the prior week.

That evening, my sister and I went to a favorite ice cream shop. The parking lot was so full that some cars were parked along the street under the trees. My first thought was to wait a few minutes for another car to leave the parking lot. Dismissing that small thought, I told myself that other cars were parked out along the street, things would be fine, and we were not going to be very long.

While standing in line, I heard the small voice within saying, "Go move your car." I dismissed it again, thinking I would only be there a short time and that I was just overreacting because I had a new car. A few minutes later, the nagging thought returned, "Go move your car." Yes, I dismissed that one as well. Finally, as my sister and I were walking out of the ice cream shop, I observed a black SUV start to park behind my car. I quickly pressed my car lights from several feet away so the driver would see my car. Fortunately, the SUV stopped. I felt relieved because he had almost hit me. Whew! I glanced at the back of my car and saw that everything seemed to be all right, so I got in and drove off.

The next morning while we were coming out of a store, my sister looked at my car and said, "Was that there before?" When I looked in the direction she was referring to, I saw the passenger side bumper had been scuffed; two small nicks were visible where the paint had been scratched to the base. Oh, my God! I had been hit last night. I just hadn't seen the side, and I had been more concerned about the driver hitting the back of my car. This story is a perfect example of how important it is to trust and listen to your small voice within.

When I shared this story with a dear friend, he pointed out that I was listening, but I had chosen not to trust that inner intuition or to act upon it. So true! I was responsible. Needless to say, when I returned home, I scheduled a body shop appointment for a new car I'd had for only forty-eight hours.

LESSONS CONTINUE

Lessons continued for me that day to make me listen to the small voice. My sister and I had wanted to visit Nob Hill on Cape Cod because we had not gotten there earlier in the summer. Wanting to be nice, one afternoon I thought we could take a trip to check it out. The GPS said it was going to take almost an hour without traffic. If we left immediately, we could get there, spend some time, and come back in the evening. My gut knew this was probably not the best time to go because we would hit rush hour traffic, yet I knew it was something my sister had set her heart on all summer. If you are familiar with the

Cape, you know summer traffic is a reality.

About forty minutes into the trip, my inner voice said, "Turn around. There will be other times." I realized in that moment that I was really trying to be nice—to please someone else, but not feeling good about it. After traveling a few more miles, I turned to my sister and said, "We need to turn around. The timing of this isn't going to work for today." My sister was very open and said, "It will be there next year." I felt such relief and realized I had been focused on taking care of her needs before mine. Needless to say, we turned around, went back over the bridge, and had a lovely dinner out.

But my story doesn't quite end there. The next morning, the news reported there had been a crash involving four cars on the bridge and that the bridge had been closed overnight. I would have been traveling back on that bridge later that evening if I had not turned around. One just never knows.

EXERCISE

Think of a situation where you listened to your intuition. What was the outcome?

_____

_____

_____

_____

_____

Think of a situation where you did not listen to your intuition. What was the outcome?

_____

_____

_____

_____

_____

What are some strategies you can use when your gut or heart tells you to give yourself some space before acting?

_____

_____

_____

_____

_____

STRATEGIES:
LISTENING TO THE SMALL VOICE WITHIN

- Commit to one daily action that will keep you following your intuition. For example, sit or lay quietly for five minutes in silence before you begin your day.

- Set an intention and take a deep breath.

- Listen with your heart. Often our head tells us one thing, but our heart/intuition tells us the truth, if we listen.

- Affirmation: *I am free to speak and act with an open heart.*

SUMMARY

As we reflect on listening to the small voice, the inner wisdom within us, we realize how often we do things for others out of habit or we hesitate because we don't want to say or do things to hurt other people's feelings. These are ingrained behaviors. I challenge you to be more aware of your thoughts and to listen what your heart says is true for you.

I realize our lives can get so busy that we are operating on autopilot, not being present to situations or conscious of why we are doing things. Taking time for ourselves to reflect, journal, pray, often become someday, tomorrow, or when we are faced with circumstances beyond our control.

Listening to the small voice starts with being aware that we don't tell our heart to beat or to take a breath. Being conscious of our thoughts, feelings, and the actions we choose in response will reflect the results we are getting in our lives.

Ask yourself, "What would be in my best interest today?" Be quiet and listen.

Chapter 4

Taking the Frame Off Your Picture

"When we are no longer motivated by fear, we understand that every moment is perfect in its own way. We no longer dread what we can't control; we learn to respect the wisdom of Spirit rather than impose our will on situations. This is the path of genuine power."
— Alberto Villoldo

One of my greatest opportunities and challenges has been being a single parent. I had never envisioned myself in this role, but my marriage to a childhood sweetheart ended in a divorce. My son Ian was two and half when his dad and I divorced, and we had shared custody. Although the arrangements worked for us as parents, in all honesty, they were not conducive for my son to receive a consistent childrearing experience. It was especially difficult for Ian to adjust between two houses, routines, and sets of parental expectations.

PARENTING

Part-time parenting was stressful. Having parental responsibilities one week and none the next was the agreed-upon arrangement with Ian's dad. Thursday nights were challenging because Ian would get anxious that the routine and his environment were changing for the next week. I grew to dislike those nights because he would often resist complying with expectations and routines and be unable to fall asleep.

As a little boy, Ian was not responsible for his parents' decision to divorce. Yet, he was significantly impacted. His dad and I loved him very much, but at times, he was placed in the middle, not wanting to disappoint either parent. When Ian was five, his dad accepted a job out of the area and moved. Visits involved meeting halfway, and a few years later, Ian being placed on planes as an unaccompanied minor to visit his dad out of state. Feeling responsible for being the daily Mom and Dad in Ian's life sometimes left me feeling overwhelmed. Even to this day, Ian refers to me as "Mops," an endearing term that merges both Mom and Pops.

Statistics show 51 percent of children today will be impacted by divorce. Whether parents stay together or apart, most try to keep some semblance of consistency for their children. As a parent, it was important for me to let Ian know the divorce was not his fault. It makes me sad to see so many children experiencing this lifestyle. In some families, it often promotes the children taking sides, comparing, keeping secrets, and being afraid to tell the truth so they don't hurt someone's feelings. The parent's feelings are not the child's responsibility, yet many children face taking on this caretaker role.

STEPPING OUTSIDE THE COMFORT ZONE

Transitioning to the full-time single parent role required clearly reestablishing daily routines and expectations with my son. Looking back, I see the impact it had on both of our lives. This restructuring was not an easy road. I knew having systems and routines was essential for our wellbeing. Between the responsibilities of maintaining a home, coordinating afterschool activities and sports, and working a demanding job, I found myself so busy "doing" life. I settled into a comfort zone and only saw how my life was inside the frame. I compared myself to others who seemed to have what I wanted rather than focusing on exploring whom Ian and I were as a family: mom and son.

A few years after my divorce, I once again had an opportunity to create a picture-perfect family. However, one day I found myself sitting in a therapist's office, heartbroken and upset after a breakup with the man I loved and was engaged to. I remember glancing over to the empty chair that represented for me "the relationship." I spoke about it like it was outside of myself. The therapist redirected my thoughts from the chair to me. He asked, "What would it look like if you could take the frame off your picture?"

At the time, Ian was six. I now thought my picture of family would never be complete again. My fiancé and I were supposed to get married in six months when everything fell apart. My ability to understand and really believe my son and I were a family unit without anyone else was not something I had focused on. I was so attached to my picture looking a certain way. Although I had extended friends and family as a support system, that was just not the same.

Moving outside of the picture of "my life" as I knew it required me to think something different was possible and not to be willing to settle. I had to develop a vision that life could be happier, more productive, and less complicated.

This experience required me to become more aware of my perceptions and belief systems and the power they had over me. It was very difficult for me to shift from what I believed was going to be my forever after to my newly framed picture.

How many times have you said "No" to an opportunity because it required you to step outside your comfort zone? Being in your comfort zone is our paradigm, what we know our life to be.

How many times have you wanted something to happen a certain way, but it fell apart, requiring you to be more courageous and take a risk to do something different?

HIGH EXPECTATIONS

My client David grew up as the firstborn of four siblings. Being the oldest can carry a whole level of unspoken expectations. Often, our parents try to follow all the rules, and they hardwire their expectations into their precious children. David was expected to be the sensible and responsible one.

On some level, David felt he always needed to be aware of where his siblings might be and what they were doing just in case of an earthquake, hurricane, or catastrophe. David lived up to his parents' dream for him. He did well in school, was nice and respectful, became a star athlete, and graduated with honors from college and graduate school. His parents were very proud. Their hard work was paying off.

However, according to David's perception, life was always being defined for him, outside of himself. David had little chance to go off the grid, make big mistakes, or dream about what he would truly love to be doing with his life. He was now expected to get a job and live the picture and pattern that had been set into motion for many years. He had his law degree and was looking for a job that matched his training. David accepted a job in a mid-size law firm. He knew how to fit in because the law partners had high expectations and wanted things to look a certain way. The work environment felt similar to how he had been raised. However, after only a few years, David started to lose his passion for having everything be so intense and stressful without any opportunities for him to be creative.

Although I truly believe things happen for reasons, when I met David, it seemed like we met purely by chance. He was taking photographs at a local nature preserve for a work presentation when we started chatting. He shared with me his portfolio of previous photos. In that moment, I could sense his excitement and the fulfillment he felt in the planning, precision, and art required to capture the essence of his photographed subjects. Yet, as the conversation continued, his voice got softer and a sense of resignation emerged that he felt stuck in his job. He was making good money, but he was still paying off school loans, and he stated that he did not see any other option.

When I asked David if he would be willing to look at how his current patterns were holding him back from having greater energy and passion for his work, he shook his head and said he just couldn't see any option other than quitting, which wasn't an option. Then I asked him, "But what if you could?

What if it were possible? Would you be willing to take the frame off the picture to see how your life could be?"

A year later, David had come to realize the creativity, passion for, and precision of his photography was also a skill set he used in his work. By sharing what he loved to do, the people at work got to know him differently. They saw him as being creative, and as he relaxed, he realized some of the pressure and intense stress he had been placing on himself to fit in, seek approval, and not speak up were lessened. Now he found a way to express his creativity and continue practicing law. He had enlarged his picture in the frame.

EXERCISE

Think of a time when you felt you wanted a different outcome in a situation. How might taking the frame off your picture have helped?

_____

_____

_____

_____

_____

Take a moment to write your story of how you would like to see things moving forward.

_____

_____

_____

_____

_____

STRATEGIES:
TAKING THE FRAME OFF YOUR PICTURE

- Allow yourself to change your mind. Think about the big decisions that require action versus trying to align to others' thinking, behavior, and lifestyles.

- Give yourself time daily for yourself. Focusing for five minutes on your breath will help you feel more grounded and less distracted. Schedule a time to exercise. Be a healthy parent to yourself and treat yourself how you would love to be treated.

- If you think you have to be the perfect spouse, parent, friend, family, or coworker, how might it look if you were not perfect? For example, if you can't get to your daughter's soccer game, you could ask someone to record a video and then watch it with your daughter later, while she fills you in on the backstory of every play.

- Affirmation: *I am far greater than my circumstances*.

SUMMARY

Taking the frame off your picture allows you to be more present and honest in your situation. It requires a level of discipline and structure I had to learn over time. When you are married, things become much more complicated because you both bring different beliefs about how to parent. Develop a clear understanding of how you and your significant other approach childrearing, managing finances and family needs, and being honest about your beliefs. Speaking up, stating your expectations, and setting boundaries all impact your relationship with your spouse and children. Children are gifts who help us learn and grow. Parenting is one of the most rewarding and hardest opportunities I have encountered.

We are responsible for our choices, and even taking no action is a decision. We are far greater than any circumstances, so we need to have courage and faith in ourselves. As I think about love and acceptance, I realize "things" are really not what is important. One might call this revelation maturity, willingness to change, or being in alignment with the higher good for all. Take the frame off your picture and try on another perspective. Are you willing to be open to that as a possibility?

Chapter 5

Believing in Yourself

"Keep your dreams alive. Understand to achieve anything requires faith and belief in yourself, vision, hard work, determination, and dedication. Remember all things are possible for those who believe."
— Gail Devers

In the mid-'80s, Diana Ross wrote a song called "It's My Turn." The lyrics spoke to my soul. I felt they were written for me. At a point in our lives, we realize we are responsible for our choices and our own happiness. However, many people often feel they will only be complete if they have someone in their life, and for a time, that was true of me. I had spent years looking for someone to fill the void I had inside my heart. Online dating was one of my options, but I got tired of feeling like I was hanging on to words on a screen. It was a rite of passage for me when I came to realize I could be complete on my own.

Remember the quote I shared in Chapter 3 from Steve Jobs? "Your time is limited, so don't waste it living someone else's life. Don't be trapped by dogma—which is living with the results of other people's thinking. Don't let the noise of others' opinions drown out your own inner voice." Having the courage and confidence to take necessary action steps aligned with what you believe in your heart to be true is often not easy, yet it is essential.

MY JOB IS MY IDENTITY

"My job is not my identity." This realization was a significant teaching for me. Work was one area where I felt needed and appreciated. I believed I was a diligent leader working with teachers who were assigned to classrooms throughout a three-county area. This structure was different from the typical school district. It was a collaborative structure and worked within component schools. I loved working with teachers and administrators to support programs for students with disabilities. Listening to their issues, concerns, and feedback fed my soul.

As time went on, I moved to other leadership positions in a local school district. Having more experience and insight, I could see there were many other areas of my life that were being compromised when my energy and time were going in one direction.

Learning to have greater balance in life is a lesson I continue to embrace.

Dr. Wayne Dyer believed we are in control of our actions and reactions. He reminded people, "Most people are searching for happiness in someone or in something outside of themselves." He believed thinking someone or something else could bring you happiness was a fundamental mistake. Instead, he said, "Happiness is something that you are, and it comes from the way you think."

When I thought about seeking happiness outside of myself, I thought a great deal about my client, Jane. She was twenty and had fallen in love with Joe because of his risk-taking, adventurous behavior, and attention and love for her. She had not dated much before she met Joe at a local pub. He was different from what she had been raised to seek in a boyfriend. Her parents didn't like Joe's cavalier attitude and told Jane she could do better. But Jane said they didn't know him. Joe was fun and made her laugh. He said he loved how beautiful and smart she was, and he liked her adventurous spirit. Her friends, however, noticed that his treatment of her was more focused on him and how she made him look good. Jane loved that he always wanted her to be dressed seductively and how he would tease her in front of his friends. She was his "trophy girl."

At first, Jane liked this attention, and she rationalized it as Joe's way to show his affection and love.

However, over the next few months, she saw less of her friends and partied more with Joe's friends. Jane was losing herself to please Joe. She now avoided her parents and came home late after they had gone to bed. Joe would get possessive when any of his friends would talk with her or give her attention. Jane and Joe began fighting, and he was becoming increasingly verbally abusive. She felt scared, particularly when he was drinking because he had slapped her on occasion in his rage. When Jane came to see me, she told me, in tears, that she knew they loved each other and Joe didn't mean to be abusive. They would always make up and make love.

This pattern of behavior continued. Jane kept it a secret that Joe sometimes struck her. Jane knew this wasn't the kind of relationship she wanted, and now her friends had drifted away from her, commenting that she deserved to be treated better. Jane didn't want anyone to think badly of Joe.

One day, Jane was talking with a guy from work. They were talking about relationships and how he and his wife would have date nights. He looked forward to Wednesday nights when they would get a sitter so they could go out and have special time together. Jane started to tell her coworker how she and Joe used to go out, but now they were spending more time at his apartment drinking and watching television. Jane mentioned that Joe got really upset if his favorite football team didn't play well. In recounting the conversation to me, Jane couldn't remember what else she and her coworker said except for his question that echoed in her mind: "He doesn't hit you, does he? Because no man or woman should hit anyone! There are other ways to release frustration and anger. You deserve to be treated with respect."

Jane was stunned and speechless. Had her secret been so transparent? She quickly responded in a protective way that Joe didn't mean it, but when things built up, he would lash out. Still, the question stayed with Jane. Driving to Joe's apartment after work that night, she felt in a daze. Joe was a nice guy. She loved him and he loved her. Didn't all relationships have difficulties?

Jane started to realize she was not respecting herself by caring more about what others thought than what was best for her. She was trying to please Joe, but it was never enough. However, her coworker's words played over and over in her mind. It took Jane over a year to leave that relationship. After she sought counseling, she realized that by carrying that secret, she was eroding her own self-worth. Although it took her a while, with support, she learned to honor her own needs and dreams.

EXERCISE

Write about a situation where you relied on people or things outside of yourself to bring you happiness or to define who you are.

_____

_____

_____

_____

_____

What one action step can you take in a relationship to help you believe you deserve more and are worthy?

_____

_____

_____

_____

_____

STRATEGIES: BELIEVING IN YOURSELF

- Seek a coach to help you identify the areas of your life most in need of your attention. Seek the support of someone who believes in you.

- Be more willing and less fearful to believe in yourself. For example, when you start to think negative or fearful thoughts, become more aware and change your thinking.

- What you think about, comes about. Write in your journal the desired ending of a situation that offers a win-win.

- Remember to post affirmations at your desk at work, in your car, on the counter at home, or on the bathroom mirror that will remind you to breathe and make a conscious decision to re-lease your constrictive or fearful thoughts.

- Listen to inspirational authors and speakers while in the car, walking, or at the gym.

SUMMARY

Emotional and spiritual development are complex, and our childhood experiences have a direct impact on how we lead and live our lives. Trauma, abuse, and emotional neglect certainly have an impact on adult relationships both personally and in the workplace.

When we believe we need to be nice to manipulate situations so we can have status, love, or approval, it directly compromises our Divine purpose on a much larger scale.

Believing in ourselves takes courage, determination, and practice. Initially, we can be supported by others to take actions, and then we must take responsibility for our own actions. What I have learned is that as we become more aware and conscious of our behavior and reflect on why we are doing things, we open ourselves up to a greater connection to ourselves, others, and to a Higher Power. By being honest and not afraid of speaking our truth, and by believing in ourselves, we are given greater opportunities to be genuine and for our authentic selves to continue to evolve. This is a lifelong journey!

When we look through the lens of our increasing belief in ourselves, we feel more empowered about making a difference in the world.

Chapter 6

Speaking Your Truth

"When a woman tells the truth, she creates the possibility for more truth around her."
— Adrienne Rich

At times, we may want to respond to a situation out of anger, frustration, or disappointment. As a child, I was often reluctant to speak up because I didn't want to get into trouble or have one of my parents or someone else be angry with me. Being told to be the "good girl" was my well-learned childhood mantra.

NOT FEELING SAFE

Have you ever been in a situation where you would have loved to say what was on your mind, but you knew it wasn't the right time or place? Maybe you felt it wasn't safe to speak up. You may have grown up believing you didn't have the right to set your own personal boundaries about what was acceptable in your life. Perhaps you tolerated sarcastic comments or derogatory jokes. As adults, we experience disappointments and even anger. Speaking up at times brings up resistance, fear, different perceptions, and angst.

When I addressed a client about the safety of using her voice, she told me, "If I said what I wanted to say to my boss or coworker, I would be fired or there would be some kind of retribution. It doesn't feel safe for me to speak up." Let's be clear; I encourage you to speak your truth, and exercising good judgment is critical. Particularly at work, it may be inappropriate to speak up in that exact moment; the timing and situation all need to be considered. But that does not mean we decide to do nothing.

SPEAKING UP

We are often afraid to speak up—perhaps because we feel stressed and overwhelmed by how our coworkers, boss, and family members may react when we do. Sometimes we first need to detach from the drama, reframe our thoughts, and then speak our truth at a later time in the day or the next day, or to discuss the situation with a trusted person who can give us unbiased support. Then we can construct an action step for addressing the situation. Coming back with a win-win situation can certainly help the situation more than blaming or complaining. One tool I recommend clients use is a journal. Journaling helps get mind-consuming thoughts onto paper to give us distance from our circumstances.

TAKING A STAND

Chris, a client, was an upper level leader in her organization responsible for implementing organizational changes for greater profit and outcomes. One day, she learned other male leaders were being hired with a higher beginning salary than she currently made. Chris had higher credentials and more experience as a leader, but she felt she was not being appreciated or valued in her job. She started to wonder if she was being discriminated against. Over time, Chris's concern consumed her until she knew she had to speak up. Having conducted her own research, she prepared a report documenting the chain of people who had been hired with less experience than she had, yet were offered a higher salary. With the report, she included a list of her job responsibilities and accomplishments. Chris then made an appointment with her supervisor to ask for a raise.

Based on their conversation and the information she had prepared, Chris felt her supervisor heard her concerns. He stated he could support her request and bring it forward to his board. A few weeks passed without any word. Chris was seething with anger and frustration. Being very attached to the desired outcome, she was outwardly becoming curt with her colleagues, and her frustration at work was beginning to spill over at home to her family. In our sessions, I asked her to visualize the outcome if it all worked out. What would it feel like if she released her attachment to the desired outcome? A few weeks later, Chris called, excited to tell me she had finally gotten her raise and had been praised for the quality of her work and the contributions she had made to the organization. She was pleased that she had been able to stand up for herself and speak her truth.

SAVING THE DAY

Years ago, a colleague was to take the lead on designing summer professional development workshops for our staff. As the date got closer, nothing had been planned or communicated to the participants. Due to my own anxiety to meet the deadline, because I was functioning in a support team role, I thought the situation would reflect poorly on me, so I stepped in to plan and coordinate the activities that needed to be completed. Today, I laugh as I envision myself as a woman with a red cape coming in to "save the day."

In hindsight, I never went to my colleague to speak my truth by saying I was anxious about meeting a deadline or angry about the role and responsibilities I ended up taking on. Instead, I took care of it and provided the "off the hook" card to someone whose responsibility it was to complete the task. Interestingly, I see I was really teaching this colleague that if they wait long enough, someone else will take care of it. And I got to be right about taking control when it wasn't my issue. Naturally, because I wanted to be nice, and I knew I needed to work with this individual, I brushed it off like it was no big deal, but it was. I let my own work lag and ended up taking things home to complete while I used my work time to do someone else's job. Although we can't roll back time, I am grateful to say, given the situation today, I would be honest and speak my truth so we could collaborate to complete the task.

WHOSE ISSUE IS IT?

Some parents may identify with the "Whose issue is it?" scenario with their own children. When my son was younger, he would sometimes wait until the last minute to tell me something was needed at school, that he had a deadline to meet for a school report, or what his financial commitments were. My knee-jerk reaction was to solve the problem rather than letting him figure it out, possibly fail, and learn to pick himself up, which he was very capable of doing.

I had to ask myself, "Why am I bailing him out?" Did my save-the-day mentality result from my own need to be needed and loved? Was I worried more about what others would think if he failed at something? Speaking up and standing my ground was overshadowed by a deep-rooted pattern of thought that my responsibility was to take care of others before myself with a payoff of feeling like a hero, loved, and needed.

If you share this pattern of thought with me, the good news is we are not unique. This behavior is not uncommon; it is often seen in individuals who grew up in a dysfunctional family. Today, many books like this one, as well as magazines, personal development opportunities, counselors, and therapists are available to help individuals and families navigate and remove themselves from dysfunctional waters. Bottom line, we get to choose how we respond in these situations. The lesson is to own the issue only if it is ours.

BEING TRUTHFUL

My client Sara was in her mid-forties when she came to see me. She wanted a love relationship and shared a story of dating a man for several months.

They had met on a blind date. She described him as quiet but wanting to please her and make her happy. She enjoyed his attention, and dinners out, walks, and movies with him. At first, she was flattered by his advances and interest, but as time went on, she often felt like she was the one keeping the conversations going and planning things to do. When I asked her, "What is your truth in this relationship?" she replied that he was a very nice man, so she didn't want to hurt his feelings by telling him she really did not see the relationship becoming long term.

Why did Sara find it so hard to tell her boyfriend she had other interests and dreams and really didn't see those being fulfilled with him? During our coaching session, I asked her what kind of relationship she really longed for. When she was honest with herself, she became clearer about what was important to her, including wanting more light-heartedness, spontaneity, and stimulating conversations. She had several interests she had put on the back burner so they could be together. Sara was not forthcoming with sharing her needs and interests. She realized that by not speaking her truth, she was feeling stuck in the relationship, and she knew in her heart that she needed to take action and be honest for both of them. No matter with whom we are in a relationship, we have to remember that the other party is not a mind reader.

BOTH BEING NICE

One morning while I was visiting Bridget, a dear friend from Michigan, she asked me whether I wanted to leave the morning news on the TV. At the time, I was taking a break from all the political drama that seemed to be on all the stations. But knowing Bridget loved to watch the news, and grateful to be visiting her, I said it was fine to leave it on. Not long after, Bridget left the room, and when she returned, she suggested we turn the television off. I laughed to myself, noticing that I had not wanted to disrupt her morning routine by turning it off, which is what I really wanted in that moment.

Although the story may sound trite, ask yourself how often you say or do things out of habit, not even listening to the question, which might change your response. What if you spoke up about what you would really like when asked? As I journey through life, I am becoming more aware of how often, out of a habit of being nice, I may not state my preference and speak my truth.

EXERCISE

When have you stopped yourself from speaking up for yourself and why?

_____

_____

_____

_____

_____

What does it cost you when you don't speak your truth with your significant other or a friend?

_____

_____

_____

_____

_____

Consider a situation where you need to have a difficult conversation with a loved one. What is one action you can take to make sure your truth is heard?

_____

_____

_____

_____

_____

STRATEGIES: SPEAKING YOUR TRUTH

- Give yourself permission to say "No." Even good people say "No."

- Intentionally pause before responding and say to yourself, "Is this in my best interest?"

- Use a few expressions to create possibility, such as, "Let me think about that," "Let me get back to you," or "That is an interesting perception or interpretation."

- Don't play small in the world to make others feel better.

- Be clear on your priorities and vision to support you in mind, body, and Spirit.

- Affirmation: *It's a joy for me to speak my truth*.

SUMMARY

As children and adults, we have all learned to keep secrets. In some cases, we learned not to tell anyone because it wasn't safe to speak up to tell our truth; sometimes we felt no one would believe us, or we didn't want to hurt someone's feelings. Today's news headlines of physical, sexual, and emotional abuse—happening to women, men, and children at home, in churches, in schools, in businesses, and in political organizations—all highlight situations where it is important to speak our truth. Speaking with heartfelt intention is paramount for our own forgiveness, worthiness, and healing. The truth is being given a voice. Speaking your truth takes awareness, courage, and the value of self.

It is amazing how every day offers an abundance of lessons. When you are assertive and clearly speak up for yourself, you are truly communicating your needs and expectations. Speaking up requires you to take time to get to know what those needs, desires, and expectations are for you and not for anyone else. It's an opportunity to release the old messages you have taken into your subconscious mind. And it takes courage and strength. As you learn to trust yourself more consistently and be comfortable with who you are, you will also learn to speak up in a way that allows you to be true to yourself.

Chapter 7

Setting Boundaries for Yourself and Rocking the Boat

"Not rocking the boat is an illusion that can only be maintained by the unspoken agreement not to feel and in the long run it never really works. Let go of saving the boat and save the passengers instead."
— Kenny Loggins

How many times have you wanted to say something but chosen not to because you did not want to create a scene or rock the boat?

Often when I've found myself in such situations, I've resorted to being nice, quiet, complacent, or non-committal, usually so I wouldn't make waves. Many of us learned survival behaviors to cope with what were dysfunctional situations. I remember my dad trying to keep the peace between my mother and me, which was often quite a chore. Many times, our home environment felt like walking on eggshells; I never wanted to say or do something that would trigger an overreaction or disruption. I spent many years as a child learning what to do to get approval. I remember my dad would just give me "the look." No words ever needed to be spoken. It was a stern, piercing feeling. I perceived it as representing disapproval and judgment, and I did whatever it took to get back into his good graces. Little kids are amazing; they are so innocent, and all they want is to genuinely feel a parent's love and approval.

SETTING BOUNDARIES

Sharon was a bright, funny, and outspoken mother. Her daughter Lynn was an only child. As a young child, Lynn appeared to be quiet. Sharon and Lynn had a tumultuous mother-daughter relationship during the rebellious teenage years and into adulthood. The dynamic from Sharon's perspective was one of loving, caring, helping, and offering suggestions. Lynn perceived her mother's attention as critical of her choices and decisions, and she would respond abruptly, defensively, and sarcastically. Their conversations were disrespectful, and it made others uncomfortable to be around them. Sharon would become embarrassed in front of her friends when these flare-ups occurred between her and Lynn.

As Sharon's friend, I could see the pain, frustration, and hurt both of them were carrying. They were holding on to the old stories that continued to separate them. Sharon loved her daughter tremendously, and eventually, there was a son-in-law and grandbaby in the picture. Lynn's comments to her mother often seemed uncalled for, while Sharon would swallow her words and thoughts to keep the peace rather than respond, or she would use humor, responding sarcastically, to get her point across.

Sharon knew her and Lynn's behavior pattern was unhealthy and creating a stressful situation for the entire family. Finally, Sharon decided, despite some fear about the outcome, to speak her truth and establish some boundaries. She expressed what behavior was acceptable, stated that she deserved to be treated respectfully, and said she would no longer tolerate abusive and sarcastic language. She knew setting these boundaries could affect whether she would see her grandson, but in her heart, she knew it was the right action. Today, Sharon and Lynn's relationship continues to heal, and they have become more accepting of their talents, abilities, and love for each other and their family.

As children, many of us learned to tell adults what they wanted to hear because we didn't want to rock the boat. It is interesting how this ingrained behavior influences our intimate relationships in adulthood, including being afraid to tell a partner or family member how we feel or just being honest. Both women and men I interviewed for this book shared that they often decide how much they are going to tell their partner, particularly if they feel it is going to be received with a negative or judgmental response. Have you ever omitted information and hoped the other person would never find out? Keeping secrets usually doesn't serve either person.

SOMETHING IS OFF

Martha and Ted were planning to get married at the end of the summer. Eight months before the wedding, Ted was offered a promotion in a city several hours from where they lived. He accepted the promotion and moved, traveling home on weekends. Martha and Ted chatted once or twice a day on the phone. Occasionally, Martha would call back later after they had their ritual evening call. Sometimes when she called, Ted wasn't home to answer the phone.

Initially, Ted's reasons for not taking Martha's call sounded legitimate. Ted would tell her stories of all the new people he had met and all the drama at his job. Martha listened with interest. Yet as time went on, Martha became obsessed with the number of nights Ted wasn't home to take her calls. Her suspicion intensified as she listened to and left voicemail messages. Ted always returned the call the next morning before he went to work. Martha's mind was consumed with feelings of wonder, concern, anger, and disbelief that Ted might be betraying their commitment to each other. When he returned home on weekends, like a scene in a movie, they acted like everything was fine. But was it? Intuitively, Martha knew something was not the same, but she attributed it to Ted's new job and travel. Still, she had a nagging feeling, and she debated whether she should rock the boat with questions.

Was Martha being honest with herself? What responsibility did she have to herself to confront her fears? It took Martha a long time to ask, "Is there someone else?" She was devastated when she heard the response; her world turned upside down. Like tearing off a Band-Aid, the pain was horrible and hurtful; her trust in herself and others had been shattered.

Martha sought outside counseling and support. Without outside support, Martha could have remained stuck in an old story of betrayal, never learning to trust again for years or even a lifetime. Being honest with ourselves is all we really have.

How many times have you not wanted to say what you were really feeling because you didn't want to rock the boat? You may have experienced this situation on a much smaller scale. For instance, this situation often happens when people are suggesting places to go out to eat. An older friend of mine had a certain restaurant she loved. We would go there every time I visited her. When I would suggest another place, she would always react with all the reasons we should go to the same place. I figured it was no big deal; it was just a restaurant, and I was being nice. I didn't want to rock the boat. However, I realized over time that it was still important to speak up and make suggestions, versus just letting it go. Sometimes we need the little situations to present themselves so when the big ones come, we are clearer with our preferences. Speaking up is like a muscle; unless we use it, it begins to atrophy.

HELD ACCOUNTABLE

Peter loved his job and his family. He loved to please others, saying it was his way of giving to them. He had a bakery manager's position at a local grocery store. He worked hard to keep the department looking presentable and to meet the health standards and codes. However, he would tell others that he felt he would never get a promotion or be assigned a bigger store because his boss didn't like him.

Tami really liked Peter as a boss; he was kind, encouraging, and respectful to her. However, she would become angry with him for not holding others accountable for their jobs. Because she worked mornings, she was frustrated that the evening crew never cleaned the food cases well or replaced the inventory. When she spoke up by explaining to Peter the extra work this meant for her, he listened, but he did not take any action with her coworkers. Peter was hesitant to speak to the evening crew. He didn't want them to quit since he would then have to hire and train new people.

Peter's refusal to make waves had a ripple effect on the crew. Tami felt frustrated in her job. Peter's boss may have recognized his lack of management skills when he did not hold employees accountable for their expected job responsibilities. Wanting to be nice and be liked had a detrimental impact on Peter and his crew.

A few months later, Tami made a decision to look for another job where she could feel her efforts were having a greater impact in her job. Tami called me with excitement in her voice because she had met a friend for dinner who had provided her with a lead. The potential job would give her greater flexibility to complete her education and still feel she was making a difference with others.

Although Tami was sad to tell Peter she had accepted another job and would be leaving, she knew in her heart that it was the best decision for her and it was not her responsibility to take care of Peter.

EXERCISE

Think of a time when you went along with someone because it was easier than having an argument or getting someone upset with you. What could you have done differently in this situation?

_____

_____

_____

_____

_____

Think of a situation when you wish you had set a boundary to take care of yourself either physically or emotionally. If a similar situation arose, what action might you take now?

_____

_____

_____

_____

_____

Take a few minutes to reflect on what relationships are like when you feel loved, honored, and respected. What will you do today to be there for the most important person—you?

_____

_____

_____

_____

_____

STRATEGIES: SETTING BOUNDARIES FOR YOURSELF AND ROCKING THE BOAT

- Take a few minutes daily to set your intention for greater peace of mind. This provides greater focus and a calmer way to start the day. Avoid reading or responding to email the first fifteen minutes of every day.

- When experiencing a disagreement or an argument, set an intention to be willing to remain calm in the conversation. Take time to assess the situation, and if appropriate in that moment, speak your truth with respect and confidence.

- Take some time to reflect on a situation. Ask a family member or coworker if you can talk about something that happened for clarification or a "do over."

- Set a certain time in the evening when you walk away from your phone and computer.

- Establish a calendar of activities, including scheduling daily time for yourself.

SUMMARY

It's time to step into your greatness and stop play-
ing small. Demystify the impact you have allowed
others' reactions to have on your behavior. Claim
your voice and set a boundary, both physically and
emotionally, if necessary. Your self-worth is built
on you taking care of you, not others taking care of
you. You are not a victim in your own life. Stop giv-
ing your power away to others. Let the boat rock
in relationships. Learn to give and embrace the gifts
of love, attention, and wonder, as well as the con-
flict and discontent. Life is all about giving and re-
ceiving, and learning to do so in a healthy way. As
Kenny Loggins said, "Let go of saving the boat and
save the passengers instead." There is nothing wrong
with taking care of you!

Chapter 8

Being Kind Versus Being Nice

"Kindness connects with who you are, while niceness connects to how you want to be seen."
— David Levithan

Plato defined kindness as being "more than deeds, it is an attitude, an expression, a look, a touch. It is anything that lifts another person." For me, the word "kind" provides a sense of heartfelt freedom—a feeling of being unencumbered. It holds power with a sense of purpose, compassion, intention, and authenticity, with no hidden agendas.

Being kind to others feels more personal than actions driven by being nice out of personal habit, how we want to be seen, or for personal gain. What do I mean by that? Being nice has been my way of integrating a way of being in the world. I learned at a very early age that being nice allowed me to stay out of trouble; get love, attention, and approval; be rewarded; and be recognized for good behavior or performance.

Mother Teresa once said, "To be kind is more important than to be right. Sometimes all a person needs is not a brilliant mind that speaks, but a patient heart that listens." Although I will always be a nice person, I have substituted the thought where appropriate to say I am kind. Being kind is heartfelt; it holds an intention of gratitude for another as a conscious choice.

BEING TOO NICE

Can someone be too nice? If you lose yourself in the process, I would say yes. Being too nice occurred for me in situations when I was not owning my voice to get my needs met, setting clearer boundaries, or being honest about my feelings and opinions. It is what prompted me on my journey to write this book. Many authors have explored the word "nice" and the effect it has on our psyche. As I started to think about the words "kind" and "nice," both began to take on different meanings for me.

Being aware and more conscious of my intentions helps me reframe my thoughts and words when giving to or receiving from others. This reframing feels different than doing something because I may have felt obligated to or out of unconscious thoughts or manipulation. Even as I write this, I pause to say to myself that I don't want people to think I am not nice. It's amazing how insidious our need is to be positively perceived by others.

When I asked a colleague what her perspective was about being nice, she quickly responded that because she grew up in another country, being nice was not a word she used to describe herself. She shared an article from the July 2015 issue of the *Journal of Judgement and Decision Making* that discusses reputations from prosocial behavior across cultures. Interestingly, the research stated that among different world cultures, it pays for one to have a reputation of being nice, but it does not pay to be really nice. This research reinforces most of our experiences growing up and practicing this learned behavior.

How often do we tell young children to "be nice"? At Christmas, we emphasize the difference between the desired behavior of being "nice" versus being "naughty." Girls and boys are told Santa Claus will not bring them presents if they are not nice. Many of us were trained from the womb that nice was an attribute to be expected or to evolve into.

When my son was growing up, I would tell him to be nice when we visited his grandparents or a friend's house. "Remember to say please and thank you" was an easy behavior, but behaviors of not interrupting the adults and playing cooperatively with the other children required more explicit directions from me than just assuming he knew what I meant when I said, "Be nice."

Years ago, as a new administrator, I super-
vised a teacher whose job required traveling from
one school to another. The teacher would submit a
monthly mileage claim that I would sign and sub-
mit to the business office. One time I was on vaca-
tion and missed the pay cycle for signing the claim.
A week later, the teacher came to me because he
was depending on that check to make a payment on
his car. I felt really bad that my absence had put his
family in this situation. I knew the payroll was on a
schedule, so having a check cut would not be an op-
tion. Wanting to be nice, I took the money out of my
wallet and told the teacher he could pay me back.
When I shared the story with a loved one at home,
the conversation was not as understanding!

Today, I would not make or recommend that de-
cision to anyone. Although the situation was unfor-
tunate, I took on responsibility for solving someone
else's problem without looking at the bigger picture.
Certainly, it would not have been condoned by any
work environment, and it was not my responsibil-
ity to bail out someone's financial obligations. Be-
cause I took on that problem, I also left myself with
less resources for that month. The kinder response
would have been to be compassionate, understand-
ing, and apologetic, but to make sure I was taking
care of me, not someone else, which ended up being
at my expense on several levels. My intention clearly
was to help someone out. If the teacher did not pay

me back, that would have made the situation much worse, and been a deeper lesson learned.

CHANGE IN PLANS

How many times have you changed your plans to be nice? "It's no big deal," you say as you comply with another person's request or suggestion. One evening, my friend and I were driving to the movies. Having some extra time before the show, she suggested we stop at a local store so she could buy something before we got to the mall. As I started going past the mall's entrance, she said she thought we could stop and get tickets before we went to the store. In that moment, I was in the passing lane and not near the turn. Yet I found myself trying to accommodate her by making the turn and slowing traffic. I realized in that moment—and commented to her in an exasperated voice, "You know, I am trying to be nice at the moment." I was aware of how quickly I went to that responsive behavior. Old patterns die hard. Reflecting back, I see we both had different expectations without clearly communicating. Very subtly, I was trying to be a good guy and please another.

You may be thinking being nice isn't a bad thing. I completely agree. Yet, when your unconscious, ingrained way of being begins to take a toll on your physical, emotional, or spiritual health, it's time to take notice. The good news is I have learned a lot from this game called life. I truly love and accept myself for being both kind and nice to my core. I love to help and get great joy and pleasure from supporting others. I am grateful that I am much more aware now of my actions and patterns and the impact they can have on me and others. What does being both kind and nice look like in your life?

EXERCISE

Think of a time you were trying to be nice by solving a problem for someone else, but it cost you more than you expected in time or money.

_____

_____

_____

_____

_____

Describe a situation where you were kind while setting a healthy boundary to take care of yourself and connect with who you are.

_____

_____

_____

_____

_____

Describe a time when you were nice because you wanted to be accepted. How did that work out for you?

_____

_____

_____

_____

_____

STRATEGIES: BEING KIND VERSUS BEING NICE

- Be kind to yourself by setting a daily intention of gratitude for your life. Choose a positive mindset for that day. For example: I am a healthy vibrant woman. I love volunteering to help others. I love and accept myself.

- Call a family member or coworker to revisit a conversation where you recognized you automatically responded just to be nice. For example, agreeing without thinking about the consequences of having a friend stay at your home for a month while they are on vacation.

- Slip a little note of encouragement into your child's backpack. Send a text or message to a loved one, wishing them a great day!

- Be willing to graciously give or receive a cup of coffee or pay for a meal.

- Instead of agreeing with someone when you disagree with someone, respond "That is your perception. I perceive it differently. That's interesting."

SUMMARY

As children, we often learned to tell adults what they wanted to hear. This behavior pattern followed most of us into adulthood. It may have become a way we communicate with the world. We assume everyone knows what we mean, and often, our intention of using our words gets perceived in a much different fashion than we imagined or intended. David Levithan offers this interpretation: "Kindness connects you with who you are, while niceness connects to how you want to be seen."

Both kind and nice are ways of being in the world. They represent how many of us act in our businesses with our families and friends. We can be kind as well as nice.

Chapter 9

Forgiving Yourself for Choices Made

"We cannot change the past, but we can change our attitude toward it. Uproot guilt and plant forgiveness. Tear out arrogance and seed humility. Exchange love for hate—thereby, making the present comfortable and the future promising."
— Maya Angelou

Looking back on my life, I often wonder, "If I knew then what I know now, how would my life be different?" Has this question ever crossed your mind? I believe all things happen for reasons. We are divinely guided. Some may say the Universe, a Divine Spirit, God, a Higher Power, or an energy greater than ourselves guides us. All of these possibilities acknowledge that we didn't get here alone.

There is clearly a Source greater than ourselves, and when we believe we are greater than our circumstances, it provides us with an opportunity to engage in life differently.

FORGIVENESS

I realized I needed to forgive myself for times when I went to my pattern of being nice rather than speaking up to be honest with myself or another. When we realize being nice is costing us our own health and wellness, it is time to forgive ourselves, let go, and move on. *A Course in Miracles* refers to forgiveness as a shift in a perception that removes a block inside me to my awareness of love's presence. I find that very healing.

Forgiveness is the art of releasing an injustice at the mind, body, or spirit level. We all carry a resentment, hurt, betrayal, or sense of guilt or shame with a focus on another or ourselves. Research has been published on this topic. According to *Greater Good Magazine*, "Psychologists generally define forgiveness as a conscious, deliberate decision to release feelings of resentment or vengeance toward a person or group who has harmed you, regardless of whether they actually deserve your forgiveness.... Forgiveness does not mean forgetting, nor does it mean condoning or excusing offenses."

I have incorporated forgiveness into my daily practices. Because injustices in this world have occurred and continue to happen, forgiveness is a tool that has taken on different meanings of thought. As a child, it was a simple good or bad, a reward or punishment. In his book *The Four Agreements*, Don Miguel Ruiz addresses the source of self-limiting beliefs and agree-ments based on family and societal programming. He offers ways of thinking and living a life that help us release the thoughts we ruminate on and that snatch our joy and happiness.

Can you remember as a child when an adult told you to tell someone else you were sorry? Often, I wasn't even sure what I had done wrong, never mind feeling sorry for it. Other times, when someone in-flicted physical or emotional pain on me, I didn't al-ways use my voice to stand up for myself and re-quest an apology from them because I didn't feel it was safe.

Some individuals I interviewed for this book re-ferred to themselves as "recovering Catholics." They have reinterpreted and questioned some of the be-liefs and practices of their religion and the impact their religion has had on them as adults. They re-called how, when practicing the Sacrament of Pen-ance as little children, they would be somewhat scared to go into what looked like a small dark booth or closet to tell a priest through a screen that they had sinned and were sorry. The priest would then tell them they were forgiven and give them a penance to say or perform. Some wondered wheth-er the priest could tell who they were because they grew up in a small town. Others laughed and said they would disguise their voices in hopes of not be-ing recognized. As adults, we all reflect on our beliefs, both their contradictions and affirmations. Every religion has a practice around forgiveness, so we internalize what is best for us.

I have noticed that having a predominant pattern of being nice, and compromising my truth, requires some personal forgiveness.

BEING AWARE

Have you ever had a particular thought or feeling that you chose to stifle just to be nice? Maybe you wanted to end an argument, or you were nervous about the response of a lover, friend, or boss, so you said nothing. Later, you went home or walked away to scarf up whatever was in the refrigerator, have another glass of wine, a bottle of beer, or a pint of ice cream. You tell yourself, "I will take the high road; it's just not worth going there." The choices I made to avoid the uncomfortable feelings beneath an altercation, or to use my voice prompted me to see that up until I became aware that I was being nice, my reactions were not serving me but impacting my health and wellness. At times, my ego justified my being nice and over-accommodating behavior rather than standing my ground and being honest about how I felt.

Today, the media is constantly informing us about health and wellness. The United States has high proportions of youths and adults with diabetes, obesity, and heart disease. Ads sell us pills for anything we can think of, and we are constantly made aware of the latest research on ways to release stress and how meditation and mindfulness can bring a sense of peace and calm to your day. With this health and wellness information at hand, I had to forgive myself for a pattern of eating and spending habits that provided immediate pleasure, but, in the long run, were destroying my body and soul's energy and vibration. Our bodies are incredible gifts. If we continue to feed ourselves processed foods and sugar, then we know these behaviors and habits will result in poor health and even debilitating diseases. When we continue to seek things outside of ourselves, we become shallow and lose our connection to our inner Source.

CHOICES MADE

Years ago, I went to one of my high school class reunions. It is always fascinating to hear how others' lives are unfolding. I struck up a conversation with Fran, my old biology lab partner. I remembered him as a bright, creative, and funny guy, but as he shared his stories, I heard a hint of sadness in his voice that he didn't have the courage to step outside of his comfort zone to pursue his dream of being an interior designer. He loved art and could put colors and combinations together so beautifully, but he was working in a stressful job as a nurse at a hospital, working long hours and taking care of his mother's house where his two brothers still lived. Although he had bought his own house, he didn't spend much time there, nor have time to make it feel like a home. I felt sad to hear about his feelings of defeat and how he regretted some of his choices not to pursue his dreams.

As we continued to talk, I gently reminded him of the good he had provided, the difference made to the hundreds or even thousands of people at the hospital, and I told him he should forgive himself for choices made that were for a higher good. We can all identify with decisions made or previous circumstances in life that have us in a different place than we expected. We can also allow ourselves to see how our lives have offered good even when we can't see it and we can be in a vibration of gratitude for greater inner fulfilment.

WANTING TO HELP

My client Patti shared with me a story about her interaction with her neighbor, Jim. Jim worked as a construction worker but had injured his back, limiting his ability to work. One cold afternoon in November, Jim came to Patti's door. She was surprised by his visit because they rarely saw each other except to give a wave on the street, even though before she died, Jim's wife had babysat for Patti's son after school for a number of years. Jim shared his struggles with Patti, humbly asking her if she could give him a short-term loan to get him through the holidays. Jim's story pulled at her heartstrings. She wanted to help and responded by offering him a thousand dollars. Their understanding was that after the beginning of the year, he would pay it back.

As months passed, Patti became increasingly angry because Jim had not paid her back. Because she drove past his house every day, she was constantly reminded that he had not kept his word. Patti only had a verbal agreement with Jim, and although she was angry with him, she realized she was even angrier with herself. She had not set up any arrangement; she had basically just wanted to help someone out and to be nice. Jim had not even asked for that much money, so why had she offered that much?

Patti felt embarrassed about what she had done so she didn't tell anyone else. She knew she needed to take some action to deal with what was beginning to consume her thoughts. After some coaching conversations with me, Patti recalled her mom would always tell her to share with others less fortunate. Patti could see this old belief was a pattern in her life that had gotten attached to being nice, over-giving, and being overly accommodating. Patti designed a plan of action that she felt offered a win-win to the situation. She contacted Jim and told him she needed repairs made on her home that she would take in place of his repaying her in cash. Jim accepted the offer, grateful that a win-win resolution had been found for both of them because he had also felt embarrassed about not being able to pay Patti back. Today, Jim and Patti continue to have a good neighbor relationship.

FORGIVING SELF AND OTHERS

In the story above, Patti knew that holding on to anger and resentment was having an impact on her attitude, health, and peace of mind. By offering a solution, she felt more empowered and able to let go of the unproductive thoughts and anger she was allowing to consume her. Patti became willing to forgive Jim and herself. This situation helped Patti become more empowered and aware of how she was spending her time and resources in other areas of her life as well. By forgiving herself, she developed greater awareness that she had control over how she related to others, and that she could set better boundaries and have clearer expectations.

Can you identify yourself as someone holding on to anger or resentments that are no longer serving your health and wellness? When I thought of forgiveness this way, it helped me see I was often looking outside myself to give or receive forgiveness. I realized one of the key people who needed forgiving was myself. I needed to forgive myself for some of the choices I had made in my life and how they had affected myself and others.

The above stories focus on individuals making choices and needing to forgive themselves. At other times, we may have been violated, hurt, abused, or mistreated by someone else. Then we are faced with the thought of forgiving another person. Can you remember as a child being physically abused by a parent or loved one? Did you ever forgive them? As an adult, have you ever had a spouse, significant other, child, or friend physically or emotionally abuse you? Keeping such abuse a secret is what keeps us stuck in the story of feeling unworthy, embarrassed, and hidden in the shadows of our own lives.

Often, it is appropriate in these situations to seek outside therapist support so we can heal. You deserve to have more freedom and peace in both your heart and your mind.

FREE YOURSELF

When we choose to use our voice to speak our truth, we become more confident and can make decisions that, ultimately, provide us with a feeling of heartfelt freedom and happiness. Carrying around our negative stories keeps us stuck in those stories. I know that I, as a child, during my marriage, and at other times, tolerated inappropriate behavior much longer than I ever needed to. When I set boundaries and forgave myself for not doing so sooner, I released the shame and blame I had around keeping secrets. Everyone deserves to be treated with respect. And that mindset starts with ourselves. What was I doing to myself? That was the most important question. Holding on to the anger and being resistant to forgiving another has a significant negative impact on our own heart and soul.

My friend Karen was angry with her sister, Ellen, for deciding she would leave her husband after more than thirty years of marriage. Ellen had already secured a new residence hundreds of miles away, leaving the house for her husband. Karen's brother-in-law had adopted her sister's son when they were first married and had been a good provider for their family. He always appeared to be helpful and caring. Karen felt her sister was being selfish and unreasonable. She was so exasperated with her sister's decisions that she stopped talking to her. I could hear her anger and resentment toward her sister's decision as she tried to help support her brother-in-law through this difficult time.

A month later, after carrying the sadness and anger in her heart, Karen decided, reluctantly, to call her sister to speak her truth of the impact of Ellen's actions on the whole family. Karen's perception of the situation was all she could see. During the conversation, Ellen shared other reasons that were not disclosed at the time she had told her sister she was leaving her husband. She had been too distressed to share them earlier.

Karen realized during the conversation that she was reacting based only on the information she had. After her conversation with her sister, she shifted her perception and had greater compassion toward her sister.

How many years are you willing to hold on to another's or your own mistakes? When will you decide to let go of all your hurts, pains, and heartfelt stories so you can take care of you?

EXERCISE

Are you willing to forgive yourself for something you have harbored that is keeping you stuck? What can you say to yourself to be less self-critical and more self-nurturing?

_____

_____

_____

_____

_____

You might feel there is someone you are not ready to forgive. But what if you could forgive them? What is one small action step you could take to move you toward that forgiveness?

_____

_____

_____

_____

_____

STRATEGIES:
FORGIVING MYSELF FOR CHOICES MADE

- Be open to knowing and believing you are perfect—you are enough. Be aware of when the need for perfectionism is driving your decisions.

- Notice the negative self-talk that is critical or judgmental to yourself or others. Replace it with a positive thought.

- Say the Hawaiian "Prayer of Forgiveness: Ho'oponopono": "I am sorry. Please forgive me. I love you. Thank you."

- Write a letter to someone you need to forgive. If appropriate, send it to the person, or burn it and release it.

- Take one small step to change your thought about yourself that is not serving you.

SUMMARY

Prior to forgiving ourselves or others, we have to become quiet with our thoughts and feelings. Acknowledge the patterns of thinking that you may have tolerated, such as minimizing your own needs, avoiding conflict, accepting less than what you deserve, feeling like a doormat, and sometimes believing others to be worthier than ourselves. Maybe we have tolerated verbal, emotional, or physical abuse from others or even from ourselves.

Make forgiving a daily practice. Become aware of the little judgments you have about yourself and others, and begin to release and let go of them. Trust that you have a greater Source of wisdom within you—a Divine Spirit to guide your thoughts, feelings, and actions.

Chapter 10

Staying in Relationships Too Long

"There is only one corner of the universe you can be certain of improving, and that's your own self."
— Aldous Huxley

Some people embrace the ebb and flow of life with greater acceptance and ease. They share the joy of being in long-term relationships and jobs that provide them with friends, satisfaction, and opportunities to grow and develop for greater freedom and fulfilment.

STAYING TOO LONG

Have you ever stayed in a job too long? In a friendship or a romantic relationship? Why is that? Sometimes one's thoughts beneath the behavior may sound like, "I don't have a choice; it's good enough; there isn't anything or anyone else; the economy is bad; I need my job to pay my bills; I stayed because of my children; I don't have enough money to go out on my own; or they really do not mean the hurtful things they do or say."

Some of my clients stay in a job they are familiar with. They know the rules, expectations, products, or systems, and they resist why things need to change. In relationships, they are afraid to address the issues honestly because they may lose what they have, lose the person, or hurt the person's feelings. However, a line exists between embracing change in a healthy way and holding on for dear life.

Have you ever wondered why some people talk about looking for someone special to spend their time with, while others proclaim they have no interest in ever meeting anyone special again? It's the old, "Been there, done that," conversation. Byron Katie would say, "Is that really true?" Katie challenges the reader to think about the truth beneath the belief of why they are thinking or acting in a certain way.

For several years, I found myself also searching for "the one." Actually, I could dedicate this book to all of the "loves" in my life because they have all taught me what I truly want and deserve. Thank you.

I once participated in a book study where we read Katherine Woodward Thomas' *Calling in "The One": 7 Weeks to Attract the Love of Your Life*. To my surprise, the book was not about how to find someone else; it was about how to reclaim, appreciate, and love myself. Really? Wow, I did not see that one coming. It is amazing how often we can get so caught up or distracted by people, places, or things that we lose ourselves.

PART OF THE JOURNEY

As a high school junior, I met a college freshman at a Boston university. We talked on the phone (texting didn't exist then) and saw each other on weekends. He was smart and funny and played acoustic and bass guitar in a small band. The following year, going off to college, I thought about being free to meet new people. At that point, I was "going steady" and did not know how to break up or use my voice to say I wanted my freedom. My mom had passed at the end of my junior year, so facing all those questions without a mom to reach out to was difficult. He was the only person I had dated. That was the beginning of me listening to my small voice, and then disregarding the thought. I was afraid to speak up; I could not seem to find the words to tell someone what I really wanted, especially if it was different from what they wanted.

So, I continued the relationship through college. I knew we differed on many things, but I so wanted to be loved and in a relationship. My mom had always talked with me about getting married, but it felt almost like I was fulfilling her dream. Even a week before we got married, I knew in my heart I should call it off. As I recall, he had written "Day of Infamy" on the calendar to mark what was supposed to be our special day. Was I paying attention? I was more concerned with what others would think. I wasn't courageous or confident enough to say "I don't want to get married." Besides, everything was planned. I had saved money during my summer and school vacations working at the telephone company to pay for the wedding photographer, flowers, and the restaurant for the reception. My grandmother, whom I loved dearly, helped me pick out my gown. It was all part of my fairytale wedding. My dad kept telling me he just wanted me to be happy. I didn't want to disappoint him or my grandmother, who had been my pillar throughout my life to this point. I had graduated from college in three-and-a-half years, and now I was getting married. Wasn't this the dream I had been saying I wanted?

Maybe I had watched too many childhood television shows about everyone being part of one great big happy family. I thought once we were married, everything would work out. We planned to live in Connecticut, where he worked as a chemical engineer at a well-known aeronautical company. I was happy that I would still be close to my dad and grandmother. Then, six weeks before the wedding, the company my fiancé worked for downsized and his job was cut. I was devastated.

The day after we got married, we set out on a very different journey to Baton Rouge, Louisiana, where my husband had found a new job in his field. On that 1,800-mile trip, I learned to drive a standard shift Fiat—not exactly a happy scene! This was not the honeymoon I had envisioned. Several months later, I secured a position as a special education teacher and began learning more about the Southern lifestyle. Two years into this movie, I was homesick, missed my family and friends, and wanted to move back north. The cultural differences and interests of the South were not aligned to my heart. My husband and I were having our struggles, but, of course, I thought changing our location would make a difference.

A decade later, having fulfilled the dream of marriage my mother and I had once held for me, my husband and I divorced. Unfortunately, our picture for an ever after crumbled. We were very young and developed different perspectives and desires as we navigated the years. One of the most special and lifelong gifts that resulted from our marriage, and for which I am forever grateful, is our wonderful, loving son, Ian. He has brought great joy, pride, and adventure into our lives.

Today, having gained more life experiences, I know enough about myself to realize I did the best I could with what I knew at the time. This fact is true for all of us, whether we have children or not. Time gives us more wisdom, grace, and opportunities for forgiveness, reflection, and many "do–overs." At least that has been my experience. In the decades since my marriage ended, I have learned how to joyfully have, avoid, or end personal and professional relationships. Some I have ended with heartache and sadness, while others have left me feeling relieved that I cut my losses.

LETTING GO OF THE SLIPPERS

Several years ago, I discussed with my coach certain relationships I had that I knew were not in my best interest, yet I was not willing to let go of. She asked me if I also could think of some object or thing I felt I could not part with.

I responded jokingly by saying I had these comfortable old slippers I had kept in my closet for several years. They were warm, fuzzy, light camel-colored suede moccasins with fur on the inside. I loved them. They were all broken in, and I wore them everywhere I could as shoes. My foot slid into them so easily. They were comfortable and stretched out; the soles were worn and the heels were all smooshed down. I even wore them inside my boots when I shoveled snow.

Looking back, there have been times when I have stayed in a relationship too long because it was comfortable, like that pair of slippers. Familiar, comfortable, showing some threads, tattered and scuffed, yet my tired feet welcomed them at the end of a long day. Even if I got a new pair as a gift, I kept them as a backup.

How do these slippers mirror some of the patterns in your life? Do you have relationships at work, or with family or friends that are comfortable, but that you would like to change? What will it take for you to feel courageous, happy, and able to speak up so you can step into your greatness and align to your Divine purpose? The clearer we are about who we are, the more fulfilling all our relationships can be.

LOVING YOURSELF

Interestingly, all my looking for someone to fill the void I felt in my life eventually made it crystal clear that I *am* enough. That doesn't mean I don't need anyone or never want another loving partnership. It means it is essential first to take care of and love myself with a mind, body, and spirit connection. The expression "Life is a journey, not a destination," takes on a whole new meaning as I appreciate, embrace, and integrate all the experiences, struggles, successes, and joys that have helped me continue to evolve.

When I discussed my feelings about relationships with a dear friend, she offered this perspective about having a new relationship: "Been there, done that; it takes more effort than it's worth." I have enough to do to take care of myself; I don't need to be involved with and take care of someone else. Why get involved at my age with someone? I am happy and enjoy my freedom.

Freedom is one of those deal breakers for me—the freedom to be myself, use my voice with love and honesty, and accept that not everyone will like what I have to say or be interested in my message. Today, I am comfortable in my own skin, and I am having more fun by not having to plan the moments. The essence of it all is to love and respect yourself. You do that by setting boundaries and knowing you are worthy of using your voice to take care of yourself, which ultimately allows you to be more present and open to loving relationships in your life.

EXERCISE

When have you paid more attention to the circumstances around you and lost your focus of taking care of yourself?

_____

_____

_____

_____

_____

If you are holding on to something or someone, what is one action you can take to create a greater sense of honesty and freedom in the relationship or situation?

_____

_____

_____

_____

_____

What keeps you telling yourself next week or next month you will say or do something? What if you took action on a heartfelt desire?

_____

_____

_____

_____

_____

STRATEGIES:
STAYING IN RELATIONSHIPS TOO LONG

- Take care of yourself first. Make healthy choices. Get a good night's sleep. Go for a walk, take the stairs, drink more water, and stay in motion.

- Listen to your own heart. Meditate and be at peace with yourself.

- Know you are deserving and worthy of vibrant health, wealth, and wisdom.

- Give yourself permission to make a different choice, and in a loving and caring way, let the other person know your inner truth.

- Listen to the small voice within you. Does this relationship have you feeling more constricted or expansive?

SUMMARY

Loving ourselves is at the heart of all relationships. As children, we learned we could make our parents and other adults happy by behaving a certain way. Love often felt outside of us and came from our parents, family, or relationships. It was something we needed to earn, grasp, hold on to, or control.

Problems get exacerbated when you don't speak your mind and in calm ways express your concerns and share what is important to you. Fear can keep us all stuck for a long time in our circumstances. As our stories unfold, they become similar when we live someone else's dream. Sometimes, although perhaps unconsciously, we sacrifice our own needs and thoughts by thinking that by keeping everyone else happy, we will be happy.

For several decades, my decisions were driven by patterns of believing I didn't have a choice or being afraid of rocking someone else's world. One of the biggest takeaways for me in writing this book was realizing how common my feelings and reactions were for women and men. The relationship we have with ourselves often gets mirrored back by other people. We are in control of our thoughts, not others.

Understanding, appreciating, and accepting who you are, and acknowledging the gifts and love you bring into the world surpass any effort or thoughts of seeking someone else to complete you. That is an illusion. Be in love with life. Being open to multi-facets of love is so much bigger to understand and embrace, and it is worth pursuing. Don't give up on it. Don't give up on yourself!

Chapter 11

Leading Your Own Life

*"Decide what you want. Believe you can have it.
Believe you deserve it, and believe it
is possible for you."*
— Jack Canfield

We are all leaders of our own lives. Take a moment to think about this statement. Do you believe you lead your own life? Do you believe you are responsible for your choices?

When I first thought about the statement, "There is a leader in everyone," I initially, focused my thinking on the statement as being job related. Upon reflection, I began to see it in a broader perspective that moved beyond physical reality to something more powerful. As children, many of us were leaders in class when we lined up for school lunch or went out to recess. As a teenager, I was captain of the color guard and had a lead role in the senior class play. Yet being a leader in the outside world beyond my day-to-day existence I perceived to be very different.

We all have an option to participate in leading others, but this chapter is about believing in and leading yourself. Being the leader of your own life requires guiding your own thoughts and actions.

SELF-LOVE

Ever wonder why we don't consciously teach children to love themselves? We voice the words, "Be loving," "Be nice," "Share with others," "Be responsible for your actions," and "Stand your ground." These words are all overshadowed with the unspoken mind thoughts of not being enough, being fearful, being afraid to speak up, experiencing tough love, or not feeling safe. Does this have to be part of life's journey?

Amazingly, we can hardly lead children toward understanding loving themselves if we haven't learned it for ourselves. And it seems like it takes many of us a long time to really understand and act on taking care of and loving ourselves. Loving ourselves does not mean being selfish or egocentric. It means saying "no" to people when it may be uncomfortable or unexpected by them, yet is in your best interest. My parents always taught me to share and be nice to others. Being a good student, sharing, and helping others were things I learned to do well. But learning to love and believe in myself with confidence and commitment has brought me more benefits than one chapter in this book could ever express. In fact, thousands of books have been written on this topic, and when you finish this book, if self-love is something you feel you need to strengthen, I encourage you to seek them out.

A coach can help you identify the limiting beliefs holding you back from pursuing your goals and can help you make those goals align with a life you love. Over the years, I have had various coaches for support. In the coaching partnership, I felt supported and held accountable as I navigated the waters needed to achieve the changes in thoughts and actions I wanted most. This allowed me to open up and listen to my most heartfelt desires and goals.

DIAMONDS IN THE ROUGH

We are all diamonds in the rough. We spend our entire lives polishing the different sides of our mind, body, and spirit to appreciate that we really are gems. Learning to love (polish) ourselves is also a way to give a loving gift to others and to the world. Have you thought about what your purpose is?

I recently coached Eileen, a woman with a wonderful gift for playing the piano. However, the inner message she repeated to herself was that her playing wasn't good enough, and she questioned whether people were really interested in listening to her play. During our conversations, Eileen began to see that her thoughts were old limiting beliefs keeping her from stepping into more opportunities to share her talents and abilities with others.

The old messages of what others have told us or what we have chosen to believe about ourselves as being true keeps us playing small in the world. The past interrupts or clouds our thinking. We then settle or feel more discontent.

Because I love to dance, I once signed up for ball-room dance lessons at a well-known dance studio. My two personal goals were to lose weight and to learn to follow. Yes, up until then, I was one of those women who wanted to lead, and that would frustrate my dance partners. The classes were fun. I learned a lot, built confidence in myself, and met wonderful people. Surprising myself, I learned dance routines for studio shows by a New York choreographer. These were things I had never thought possible.

Many dancers pursue formal dance competition opportunities. Thoughts of performing in that venue brought me a high level of anxiety, which distracted me from what I really wanted: to enjoy social dancing. Four years later, while continuing to take lessons, I had to be honest and assess that I was basically paying to dance with my dance instructor. The good news was I had released some of my perfectionistic thinking, learned to follow, lost weight, and could now dance socially with less pressure while having more fun.

CIRCUMSTANCES ARE LEADING ME

One of my previous life patterns was to spend a lot of my time living life as if life's circumstances were greater than I am. I was just staying afloat, trying to navigate through balancing relationships with my family and work colleagues while wanting more time, money, and freedom to make a greater difference in the world. I was very grateful for all the opportunities and the people who loved, supported, and encouraged me. However, while my life was good, it just was not as fulfilling or enriching on a soul level. I had become caught up in the routine of the day, the week, and the years. Everything seemed to be creating and serving as a distraction from believing in my dreams.

What would I truly love to do? Did I believe I deserved to have more than the life I had created to date? It seemed easier and more comfortable to be there for others than to satisfy myself. I knew the caretaking role and had mastered it well. But I felt the time had come for me to have a sense of freedom and joy. I was feeling more on autopilot than joyful and passionate about my life. As a result, I became comfortable with quieting my voice, and my true desires, I noticed, lay dormant.

My focus on my career, friends, and raising a son started to shift. I had great satisfaction in my job, and wonderful friends, and my son was now older, living on his own, and married. I was now an "empty-nester." My dad and stepmom were aging, requiring more time and attention, which often meant traveling three hours back and forth, initially to their home, but later to a skilled nursing facility. I was so grateful for my siblings who lived close by and gave my parents their utmost care and time until they passed on.

I had often compromised my relationship with myself. I was not eating in a healthy manner or exercising consistently. I began noticing I was spending money on others or things to fill a void that felt like an abyss. On some level, I knew empowerment and feeling joy and freedom were about building my own self-esteem and confidence to speak up and speak my truth. But I didn't quite see how I was going to empower myself in situations and circumstances that were often running me.

CHANGE IS CONSTANT

One fact about change is that it is constant. As things around me were changing, some days I felt like a drifter, not connecting to a clear vision of the dreams I still had in my heart, but had book-marked for later. In the past, I had often responded with black and white thinking; gray was not as comfortable. At times, I felt overwhelmed or uncertain. I would often disconnect from situations, throw myself into work, stay busy, work harder, sign up for more programs, try more diets, and read more books looking for an answer. I avoided looking within myself to ask the hard questions: What is right for me? What would I love? Where would I like to work? With whom would I like to have a loving relationship? My trust and belief in a power greater than myself, which I choose to call God, gave me comfort. (Others may choose to call this power the Universe, Divine Source, Higher Power, or another name; my intention here is to honor whatever speaks to your soul.) I learned that the more I felt separate, different, or not fitting in, the further I felt from Source. A deep yearning to connect with God led me to be more reflective and willing to look inside myself. When I trust on a Universal level, I am guided. When I tap into my intuition and listen to those gut responses, I feel more grounded and centered in my day.

When I try to figure everything out, please others to be nice, or stay focused on the problem, I become more distracted and am less productive. If you take a step back, take a deep breath, and are open to looking at things from a different perspective, it is amazing what a difference it will make for you.

Having a morning and evening practice of prayer, gratitude, and meditation provide me with a level of peace. I am happy to say I have embraced this practice as a way to be open to the changes and miracles possible in my life if only I am willing to listen to my inner voice and do the footwork.

EXERCISE

What does being a leader in your own life look like?

_____

_____

_____

_____

_____

What is something you know you could do that, if you did, would make a huge difference in moving you toward your dreams?

_____

_____

_____

_____

_____

Commit to taking one small action step, such as drinking more water, exercising regularly, or taking a deep breath when you feel over-whelmed.

_____

_____

_____

_____

_____

STRATEGIES: LEADING YOUR OWN LIFE

- Read some personal development books to help with more empowered choices in leading your life.

- Write down your daily spending. Find a financial advisor or seek out support to put a plan in place for your finances.

- Write a letter to yourself, or journal the negative feelings, doubt, or fear you are still carrying that does not serve you. Be willing to release them. Commit to thinking positively about something that will help you have a healthier attitude about yourself or another.

- Find an accountability buddy or coach to help support you in releasing patterns of behavior such as smoking, overeating, and overspending.

- Affirmation: *What I say does matter*.

SUMMARY

We can all change our perspectives and expand our awareness to greater possibilities. We can release the old messages that have kept us shackled to thinking we are undeserving or fundamentally flawed and incapable of doing things that are possible for others but not us. When we are conscious of our breath and align our energy with positive thoughts and a belief that we are already whole, healthy, and well, we truly become leaders in our own lives.

Embrace the realization that you are responsible for what you create in your life. At times, this truth may not be easy to admit, but stepping up, taking risks in your jobs, loving your relationships, committing to eating healthy food and exercising regularly, and being more financially disciplined will provide you with greater confidence and a foundation of believing all things are possible.

Chapter 12

Letting Go of What No Longer Serves You

"Letting go isn't about having the courage to release the past; it's about having the wisdom to embrace the present."
— Steve Maraboli

The majority of us learn best visually. We like to understand and see how things work. Imagine you're a cross-country skier, standing, poles in hand and boots toe-clipped to skis in a track of packed snow. You can move and stay in this track until something comes along that causes you to go off the trail. Like the trail, our routines in life are like grooves that over time become deeper and more defined, making it harder to shift course.

How do you think about and approach things in your life? Are you on the path swooshing along, accepting the way things are, and possibly not even thinking you could be living any differently? Some might say we are sleepwalking through life, and on some level, we are unconscious. As obstacles come up, some respond to living day to day by settling for being stressed and disappointed in themselves and their circumstances, without believing or imagining that things could be different.

MISSING ALL THE SIGNS

Have you ever wondered why we are not honest with each other, no matter what?

Like tearing off a Band-Aid, admitting the truth can sometimes feel horrible and hurtful. Yet, the lies, pain, and destruction of trust in oneself and in others only magnifies when we hold on to what no longer serves our highest good when we hide the truth. Without some outside support or coaching, we can stay stuck in an old story or fantasy for years—even a lifetime. It's time to be honest with ourselves. That is all we really have.

Allan and Paula had been coworkers for a number of years. They shared the same lunch period together, worked on some projects together, and enjoyed each other's company. They both liked to go to the gym and to cook. They would share recipes and sometimes go to each other's apartment to cook and have dinner. However, Paula was not interested in Allan romantically. She thought she had been clear about her desire for a platonic relationship and enjoyed their friendship. Then Paula started to notice Allan being more attentive to what she was wearing and how attractive she was. Initially, she missed the signs of his interest. She would laugh it off and thought he was just being nice. Allan even said she would be a great catch for a great guy.

When Allan began asking Paula what she was doing on upcoming weekends, she began to feel uncomfortable with his increased interest in her dating life. Paula admitted that Allan was a nice guy, that he was easy to be with, and that he always listened to her and was there for her. Now she felt his interest was more than she wanted. Because they worked together, Paula was not sure how to distance herself from this relationship, which she had also nurtured. She was afraid to tell Allan that his sweet attentiveness was feeling awkward for her.

Initially, Paula's response to Allan's invitations was to say she was busy. However, this left a nagging feeling in her heart because she knew she was not being honest with herself or Allan.

A few weeks later, Paula, who had been avoiding her exercise class, asked Allan if he was willing to get a smoothie after his workout at the gym. During their meeting, Paula gained the courage to be honest and share with Allan that she had missed and ignored some of the signs he had been sending her way, and although the relationship felt comfortable and safe for her, she was not being fair to Allan and did not want to lead him on.

They both admitted they enjoyed each other's company, but had been somewhat unskilled in communicating honestly. At this time, they felt so good about the conversation that they agreed to continue as friends with no other agendas.

NOW WHAT?

I was having lunch with Sam, a colleague who was preparing to retire from a career he had given his heart and soul to for more than forty years. We talked about how attached he had become to the work environment and culture. He knew the people, their stories, and how to respond. Everyone relied on his knowledge in getting the job done, solving problems, and being a pillar in the organization. Sam's concerns were similar to those of others entering retirement: What will I do now?

Sometimes, we are so mentally attached to circumstances that we can't imagine our life looking any other way. I encouraged Sam to think about what he would love to do. He decided he could look into the boxes of old model trains in the cellar. He used to love collecting trains and thought he might possibly start selling them on eBay. Sam also wanted to give back to his community, so he decided he would volunteer one day a week at a local food bank. Sam felt more empowered as he thought about activities he would love that would give him a sense of freedom and purpose. Taking one small action each day helped Sam stay in action. Designing a plan led to greater satisfaction and fulfillment for him.

SOON-TO-BE EMPTY NESTER

Amanda came to see me when her daughter, Joy, was a high school junior. Until then, Amanda and Joy had had a close relationship. They had begun attending college nights sponsored by the school and setting up visits to a few colleges during the weeks of winter and spring vacation. Initially, they both enthusiastically discussed potential school majors, school programs, locations, and living arrangements. Amanda was thrilled to be involved in these decisions with her daughter.

However, Amanda became anxious when she noticed Joy was investing less time and energy in talking about schools and was procrastinating on completing the college applications and other pre-admission requirements to meet the deadlines.

As Amanda and I spoke, she realized she needed to step back and let go of her own anxiety and concerns about what would be the perfect school for her daughter. She had been asking Joy daily about what action she had taken, creating more resistance and discourse between them. Amanda said she knew her behavior was not the answer, but she could not seem to help herself. In our meeting, we discussed her daughter's strengths and identified other situations where Joy had been very responsible and completed deadlines.

Later that week, Amanda reported that she had been honest with Joy about her own fears and concerns about her moving away to school, and she realized some of her excitement and input were aligned more closely to what Amanda wanted versus Joy. Amanda's speaking up allowed Joy to speak more freely about her own thoughts and desires versus trying to please her mother. Amanda agreed to listen more closely about the characteristics each school presented for Joy, and they discussed how important it was for Joy to feel good about the decision. Together, they made a list of non-negotiables and desires before they went to visit each school. This process allowed Joy to be actively involved in thinking about what kind of school and environment she would love and how the schools they had visited compared to her ideal. Together, they designed a list of the pros and cons of each school to narrow their search. Amanda knew she still had some time before becoming an empty-nester, so she decided to stay focused on first things first.

BEING TRUE TO YOU

Everyone has stories about difficult and awkward romantic relationships. In our relationships, we need, deep in our core, to be clear and honest with ourselves. What kind of relationship would you love? What is really important for your soul? When you are really being honest with yourself, then enjoying your own company, such as occasionally having dinner and a movie by yourself, is a healthy action.

If we don't set a vision for ourselves, we can find ourselves surprised when things don't work out, or we may feel like we are settling. You may even experience situations when your heart is open but the one you love and care about deeply may not end up being your forevermore. The initial hype, euphoric energy, and heartfelt connection that drive the dynamic duo help you to learn more about yourself and reassess what is important. Over time, a couple's heartfelt connection either grows together and you are on a new journey, or you both grow separately. When separately happens, you often have to decide to choose you.

DECLUTTER

If you don't love it, throw it out! Have you heard this statement? How many books or magazines have you read or purchased about the strategies for letting go of "the stuff" in your life? What are you holding on to?

I believe that what we hold on to often holds us back from moving forward more freely. Negative thoughts and attitudes or old resentments are just like the clothes we think we might wear or fit into again, magazines we save to read someday, stuff in the junk drawer, and all those little screws and gadgets that come with putting up blinds in your house that you keep but never use. I always smile when my son visits and checks the expiration dates on the jars in the refrigerator. Seems like there is always something we can let go of!

One spring, a huge rainstorm caused a flood in my cellar. I was grateful to our friends for their help saving our belongings and to the fire company that came to pump out the water. And it was a forced opportunity to declutter the cellar since there was significant water damage. Initially, I was heartsick thinking of everything that would have to be thrown out, but today, I do not even remember what most of those things were.

Dr. Wayne Dyer, a renowned personal development author, told a compelling story on one of his audio programs about his office library having thousands of books or more from floor to ceiling. He had been attached to them for years. Many were first editions or gifts. One day, he decided to have all the books packed up. It was time to let go. He wanted to be open for more freedom and expansiveness. That story has always stayed with me. One of my passions is reading self-development books and books on current educational trends. Although I have given away hundreds of books within the past year, I must confess I still have numerous books on my office bookshelves and in boxes in the attic and cellar. The next opportunity is up to you and me. Are you ready? It's time to let go.

EXERCISE

What are five things you can declutter in your home/apartment or office that would be the first step to letting go of "stuff"?

_____

_____

_____

_____

_____

Identify someone or something that has been draining your energy and joy. What can you do to let go of that thought?

_____

_____

_____

_____

_____

What is one step you can take to address that area of concern?

_____

_____

_____

_____

_____

What is one limiting belief that no longer serves you to hold on to?

_____

_____

_____

_____

_____

STRATEGIES:
LETTING GO OF WHAT NO LONGER
SERVES YOU

- Get quiet. Go inside to your inner Spirit-self. Ask yourself: What is mine to do?

- Letting go of our fear requires courage. Replace fear with faith.

- Act, trust, and believe in yourself. As appropriate, use a calendar to set appointments and schedule tasks that require confidence and determination.

- Give yourself permission to re-choose.

- Declutter; start with a drawer, closet, or one room.

SUMMARY

All relationships are about communication. As we practice becoming better communicators, there will be less unnecessary discourse. We will feel greater freedom in owning our voices, greater understanding of others, and greater love. When we are unhappy with ourselves, our relationships become strained and life feels less abundant and fulfilled.

It is fascinating how we collect things and hold on to limiting beliefs and other thoughts that don't serve us. Often, we get so busy with our day-to-day lives and activities that we don't take the time to notice what might be preventing us from moving forward with greater joy and happiness. The actions we can take to remove and release stuff in our lives is often easier than the thoughts that keep ticker-taping in our minds. When you place your focus and energy on the positive, being honest and true to you, a door for greater possibility opens. Take that step!

Chapter 13

Being Courageous and Free

*"Our deepest fear is not that we are inadequate.
Our deepest fear is that we are powerful beyond
measure. Your playing small does not serve the
world. There is nothing enlightened about
shrinking so that other people won't feel
insecure around you."*
— Marianne Williamson

One evening, when I was sixteen, after making tea for my mother who had been ill at home for a number of years, I returned to our living room to find her not breathing; she had died peacefully on the couch. The moment was surreal. It was nothing anyone wants to experience, particularly a sixteen-year-old who is home alone. My thoughts swirled with memories of all the times I had said things to her that were unkind and hurtful and all the times I had just wished she would go away. Now my heart filled with love as I felt the devastating loss of a mother I had truly adored. It had been a frustrating number of years, and I felt powerless as I watched her not take care of herself and refuse to go to a doctor. Now a huge part of myself was gone.

Many wonderful friends and family dropped off food to the house and offered support to my father and me. Yet, shortly after the wake and funeral, everyone returned to their everyday routines, while mine would never be the same. I remember someone saying, "You will need to be courageous and take care of yourself and your dad." But I felt alone, angry, and lost.

I was at a loss of what to do as I faced my junior year of high school. My teenage years with my mom had been tumultuous with a lot of arguing as I tried to own and use my voice to express what I believed, wanted, and desired.

I was in the stage when most teenagers and young adults are exploring the world, finding out who they are and what they believe, while challenging what others think as they navigate the world. Although my mom was gone, I now wanted to feel protected, so I anchored my thoughts and behaviors to many messages and beliefs my mother had instilled in me. I felt doing so was a way to honor her. Tapes played in my mind that said, "What would others think?" and "Be the good girl; be nice; don't create waves. Give to others; take care of others." My perception was that I was responsible for others' happiness, which related directly to my happiness.

These experiences and patterns of thought would determine the direction of my life as I navigated new territory into adulthood. I know some of my mother's beliefs and messages served me well by keeping me from veering off into risky behaviors in my college years like drugs, cigarettes, and alcohol that I could have chosen, and which would have brought me down a totally different path. It was time for me to be courageous and responsibly free.

MAKING THE FIRST MOVE

Growing up in a family of four, Susan was referred to as the emotional one. One Christmas Eve when she and her adult siblings had families of their own, Susan needed some help in the kitchen and asked her niece to help. Her niece erupted negatively. Susan felt disrespected and embarrassed in front of other family members, including her adult children. Donna, Susan's sister and her niece's mother, with whom Susan had a close relationship, quickly defended her daughter, saying it wasn't Susan's place to direct her. Susan felt distant the remainder of the evening to her niece and sister. On the way home, she felt hurt, angry, and in disbelief that her sister wouldn't listen to her when she tried to explain what had happened and had basically blown her off. No communication transpired between them throughout the holidays, and the awkwardness was more than Susan could bear. Although Susan felt she had not done anything wrong and her sister owed her an apology, she decided to make the first move by crafting a text, simply stating she loved and missed her sister.

How often have you been in a situation where you felt someone should be taking some action and didn't? What was your response? At the end of the day, were you left feeling more upset and annoyed? As Winston Churchill said, "A pessimist sees the difficulty in every opportunity; an optimist sees the opportunity in every difficulty." What would be a healthier action for you to take for your own health and peace?

WHEN BEING LOYAL KEEPS YOU STUCK

I met Juanita, a wonderful woman in her early forties, on a flight headed to Detroit. She commented that she travels a great deal while working in corporate America. As she sighed and got settled into her seat, I sensed she was very tired and stressed. Juanita stated her work schedule was negatively impacting her husband and children. She could not see any way to get out of the rat race since she was the family breadwinner. Her husband was on work disability. I asked her what she would love to do if things were different. She replied that she knew she could have greater opportunities if she would consider moving to another department or division.

Juanita told me she had worked for her boss for seven years, and she felt bad and disloyal even to consider leaving her job. She worked hard more than eighty hours a week between the office and snatching time at home on the weekends. In her role, she supervised many coworkers to support the department in meeting its monthly and quarterly goals. Feeling pressure from her boss to keep the department moving forward, she felt tremendous responsibility, not wanting to disappoint him since he was kind and depended on her. As Juanita concluded, her voice trailed off, saying things would be all right. She could not envision leaving what she knew.

In this situation, what was Juanita's drive to be loyal to her job and her boss costing her? What might have been possible for her to have more freedom while still being responsible to herself and her family? Allowing yourself to consider something different opens your mind to greater opportunities and freedom. What if you could?

BEING COURAGEOUS

After retiring and having more time on my hands, I wanted to learn how to speak Spanish. I knew the best way to learn would be to sign up for a language immersion program. There were a few local college programs, and I had a yearning to go to Spain. I had never traveled abroad and I was going solo. I enthusiastically started researching international programs and found a company, Amerispan, that offered immersion programs in several countries and languages. I chose Barcelona so I could have a cultural experience of seeing Gaudi's works throughout the city, including the famous Basilica de la Sagrada Familia.

I went to the library to sign out an English to conversational Spanish book. I was also grateful to have a friend who taught me a few of the essentials, like asking for directions, bathrooms, and other basic vocabulary.

When I look back on the experience, I realize I took a huge step of courage in going to Spain. Up until then, I was not a fan of even taking the train into New York City, never mind a plane to another country!

My host family experience was with Luisa, a grandmother of two elementary-age children she watched before and after school, and two other adult students from France and Belgium. Once I landed at the airport, I found a taxi, and the driver took me to Luisa's house based on the address I had written on an index card. I was excited for my new adventure but scared that I really had no clue what I had really signed up for. The taxi driver dropped me off at the house. Then teeter-tottering with a huge suitcase and a tote, I managed to get up the sidewalk. Luisa had an astonished look on her face, thinking I was staying for six months versus three weeks in a small-sized student room. I think I had overpacked.

Luisa was able to communicate that she only spoke Catalan Spanish, which was a different Spanish dialect than what I would be learning. My isolated words were not helping me, so my pocket dictionary became my new best friend.

For the next three weeks, I took the train to class in the morning with cultural field trips on the weekends and after school. The trip was quite an adventure. I learned I had to be more courageous and trust more since I could not control what I did not understand.

My seven classmates were all young enough to be my children, and it was amazing how many languages they all spoke since they came from several different countries.

I am so grateful for these experiences because they helped me to grow, learn more Spanish (which I realized you lose if you don't practice), and make some wonderful friends with whom I am still in contact.

EXERCISE

Reflect and write down one situation in your life that requires courage for you to act. What is it costing you not to?

_____

_____

_____

_____

_____

What would your life look and feel like if you had less stress and more freedom? What is one action you can take in the next fifteen minutes to support you in that direction?

_____

_____

_____

_____

_____

When have you experienced needing to be courageous?

_____

_____

_____

_____

_____

STRATEGIES: BEING COURAGEOUS AND FREE

- Give yourself permission to explore what life would look like if you felt courageous and free.

- Respond to requests from your heart that come from a place of love.

- Design a vision board focusing on "What I would love in mind, body, and spirit."

- Affirmation: *It is safe for me to be courageous and free.*

- Listen to someone else's story of courage that inspires you to think and act more confidently.

SUMMARY

It takes courage to let go. It's a part of life's process and purpose. We are ever growing and evolving. We all have family, friends, coworkers, communities, pets, jobs, or possessions that we may have attachments to and love dearly. I have come to realize that all things happen for reasons, even if in the moment, they feel horrific and bring deep sadness.

Leaves let go and fall from trees. They came and served their season. We all have reasons, seasons, and lifetimes. We are all divinely guided by a Source greater than ourselves. Enjoy being with the people in your life today. Relish the memories—some wonderful and some challenging—as you breathe into the courage of life and the freedom to be you.

Chapter 14

Taking Care of Yourself First

*"You will never change your life until you change
something you do daily. The secret of your success
is found in your daily routine."*
— John C. Maxwell

Have you ever said to yourself and to others that
you wanted to achieve a goal, but you lost momen-
tum? You know—lose weight, reorganize the office,
plan and cook meals ahead, start the taxes earlier,
write a book, start an exercise program? As I became
more aware of my thoughts and patterns, I noticed
when I set a goal that the old familiar pattern would
creep into my thoughts. This was not the first time I
had started something but never made it to the fin-
ish line. Examples include my diet and exercise pro-
gram or even an intention of writing a different book
twenty years ago. Why is that?

While writing this book, I experienced feeling
stuck. I could not seem to focus or get out of my

own way. Yes, we may all share some similar excuses, distractions, and behaviors that keep us from achieving a goal. I would schedule time daily with an intention to work on writing a chapter, then become distracted with the other to-dos in my life. This was a similar story to when I said I wanted to exercise more and have better health. Why were my actions not aligning with what I said was important and what I wanted?

A number of years ago, I had the privilege of hearing John Maxwell, a renowned leadership expert and author, speak at a leadership convention in Texas. John's down-to-earth message spoke to my heart. He offered stories and examples of how everyone starts somewhere with focused attention on their intentions, acting with purpose and commitment. His message was simple, yet powerfully complex. "You will never change your life until you change something you do daily. The secret of your success is found in your daily routine." I am ever so grateful for his message; it has helped me as a leader both professionally and personally.

I am inspired by individuals for whom a structured daily routine comes more easily. I realize my desire for a sense of freedom has often distracted me from being consciously disciplined. Success requires a positive mindset, being committed to a vision, and believing in possibilities. By thinking about what I would say to a client, "Where in your life have you experienced the same feeling and taken a different action and been successful?", I reflected on times when I released fifteen pounds, got into an exercise routine, or finished my doctorate. The consistency of my actions and my belief proved it was possible, one day at a time, to make a difference.

GAME-CHANGER

Keeping my word to myself was the game-changer. It started with small actions: drinking a certain amount of water daily, walking so many steps daily, reading something inspirational at night and in the morning, writing five gratitudes from the day in my journal, and writing at least thirty minutes daily. Up until then, I had not always kept my word to me, letting the needs of family, friends, and work come before my own. It felt so much easier to take care of them than to take care of me. Most of us can relate to that behavior. We all read books, magazines, and blogs about how important it is to take care of ourselves. If we stay in action with the vision before us, then we can trust that with patience and consistency, we can prevail, and results never lie.

To see the results I most truly desired, I chose to look for supports that would help me stay accountable to my vision for a healthier and more vibrant life.

KEEPING THE DATE

My goal became to complete writing so my experiences could inspire others to use their voices to take care of themselves with greater conviction. Using coaches, accountability buddies, gratitude journaling, food and exercise apps, and scheduling time for myself that was non-negotiable helped me be the action that made the difference.

I've asked many people to identify one action step in their daily discipline that has supported them in feeling and being successful. Several responded by saying they knew they needed to do something, but they had a myriad of reasons for why they were not. Everyone stated their health and wellness was essential. Yet their words were not aligned with their actions.

Those who appeared to be demonstrating success described their daily discipline as committing to the actions that would help them attain their most desired results. These disciplines included, in the area of vibrant health and wellness, carrying less weight, having more flexibility, and creating healthier eating patterns, which all place less mental and physical stress on the body. They learned to keep their word to themselves by going to the gym or walking even when the snooze alarm was calling, or choosing foods with more greens and less sugar.

CHANGING THE ROUTINE

Samantha had a high blood pressure scare at age thirty-two. At the time, she was a mother of two, working full-time to help pay the mortgage on her house with monthly credit cards that were close to their limit. She and her husband both worked. Finding babysitting money and going back to school were creating great stress and anxiety for her. She knew she wanted to do something to take care of herself. Samantha also knew her dad had experienced a heart attack a few years ago that had changed his ability to care for his family in the manner he desired. Samantha knew she didn't want to end up in the same situation.

What options did Samantha have to help her get off this merry-go-round? What were some small steps that might help her feel better about herself? Samantha realized taking a lunchtime walk could help shift her thoughts from some of her work frustrations. Packing a lunch versus going out saved money and allowed her to eat healthier. She spent more time on Sunday nights planning out the meals for the week so that the evenings she came home, she knew what was planned. Samantha began to feel more in control of taking care of herself and more confident, which allowed her to feel more at peace with herself at home and at work.

USING YOUR VOICE

One evening, I was invited to my friend Ann's house for dinner. As she was preparing the meal, Ann asked me if I wanted sweet or white potatoes. I responding by saying sweet potatoes. She proceeded to ask whether I was sure, and that she could cook both. We could split the two choices and have half of each. I just smiled. This time I said, "No, sweet is perfect." A few years earlier, I would have had a conversation in my mind thinking that I wasn't being heard, or that if Ann wanted a specific kind, she should not have asked! I laughed to myself when I realized that so often we are given choices, but instead of truly speaking up to say what we really want, we settle and may hold a private conversation of annoyance.

Have you ever experienced someone asking you repeatedly if you want something more to eat after you have already responded? Women often follow this pattern, perceiving it to be hospitable. I think we women are taught this behavior from an early age. Maybe it is one way "being nice" looks?

One night, prior to seeing a movie, a few friends and I decided to grab a bite to eat at a local Greek diner. As the young waitress took our order, she shared that it was her first week on the job. Three of us ordered salads and one ordered a grilled cheese sandwich without fries. In a very sweet way, the waitress asked the person ordering the grilled cheese sandwich whether they were sure they didn't want fries, and she repeated the question not just once, but three times. When the waitress returned to the table to check on us after bringing our order, it was clear that the grilled cheese sandwich was eaten, so she offered to bring something more for the individual. Her relentless need to be accommodating no longer felt sweet but was becoming annoying. We dismissed her behavior as the result of her being new and trying to please. However, later I realized her pattern of service had likely been learned long before her employment.

SCHEDULE YOURSELF FIRST

We usually think about paying ourselves first in reference to money, but the topic is far greater than that. Some people might say it is selfish to put yourself first. However, if you do not schedule some time for you, over time you will feel depleted or an illness will arise to get your attention.

It has been a journey for me to give myself permission to take care of me first and to own my voice for greater freedom and fulfillment. These actions have not always been easy, but they have been essential for my health and wellbeing. Mary Morrissey suggests when you are worrying or have fear or doubt about something you don't have control over in the moment, to make an appointment on the calendar in three days with your fear and doubt. I love that strategy because it has allowed me to free up my thoughts, knowing I will be able to focus on my fear and worry when it is reflected on my calendar. Often, I have found that in three days, the circumstances have changed and the worry and doubt that would have consumed my thoughts were freed up in my mind.

EXERCISE

What is at least one thing you do or that happens to you that distracts you from taking care of yourself?

_____

_____

_____

_____

_____

How long has that been a habit for you? Why do you want to change it now?

_____

_____

_____

_____

_____

Commit to yourself today. What is one action step you can take that will nurture your mind, body, or soul, based on what you would love for yourself?

_____

_____

_____

_____

_____

STRATEGIES:
TAKING CARE OF YOURSELF/PUTTING YOURSELF FIRST

- Seek a buddy to exercise with. Set a time to walk, go to the gym, and/or do yoga, and hold each other accountable.

- Pay attention daily to your conscious breath for at least 5-8 minutes. This is an excellent tool to refocus you when you find yourself becoming anxious, disengaged, angry, or upset.

- Write 3-5 things in your journal that happen each day for which you are grateful. Reference them periodically over the course of a week and month to help anchor the love in your heart.

- Spend time on the weekend preplanning the coming week's meals.

- Say "No" when you know you are doing something just to be nice.

- Schedule times on the calendar for yourself, such as time to walk or prepare meals. Set your calendar with a focus on attention to your intentions.

SUMMARY

Commit to yourself. Give yourself permission in baby steps to put your own needs and wants first. Health and wellbeing, happiness, love, abundance, and gratitude are some of the cornerstones for taking care of yourself. On airplanes, the safety message always tells you to put the drop-down air mask on yourself first before you put one on your child. We can't help anyone if we don't help ourselves first, so why do we resist taking care of us?

The first step in the process of self-care is being honest with ourselves. We deserve to be healthy, abundant, and fulfilled. We need to prioritize what is important and identify the vision of what we most want as we create a life we love living. We need to be willing to change by being responsible for ourselves versus complaining about our circumstances and holding resentments toward others. Our lives can provide much greater freedom and happiness when we stop long enough to say a big "YES" to us.

A special message for women as well as men is to know that by getting quiet, listening to your inner wisdom, and owning your voice with truth, you will support your health and wellbeing in all areas of your life. Having faith and believing we are far greater than any of our circumstances starts with your Source and yourself.

Chapter 15

Asking for Help

"Ask for help not because you're weak,
but because you want to remain strong."
— Les Brown

In the past, women often made comments about men who resisted asking for directions. Of course, that was before we all had some sort of GPS on our phone and in our car. It would be interesting to know whether these devices have reduced the number of arguments while driving.

Have you ever experienced being afraid to ask for help? I love Les Brown's quote, "Ask for help not because you are weak, but because you want to remain strong." This perspective comes into play as you listen to your intuitive side—also known as a gut feeling or the small voice within. And then based on what your intuition says, you act.

Most of us remember times as children when we wanted something and asked our parents or a friend to help us out. Sometimes as children, we got the "desired thing," and other times, the adults in our world wanted to teach us lessons about being responsible, planning ahead and making good choices, so we were told not to ask. As adult children, some of us are still learning these lessons by not seeking help when we need assistance and support. Yet, we want to teach our children lessons about being responsible, planning, and making good choices.

Joan was my friend's sister. She had not been feeling well for a number of weeks. She would complain of being tired, having low energy, sleeping poorly, and not feeling like eating, but she was afraid to go to the doctor. Her sister called her so often to see if she had made an appointment that Joan began avoiding her calls. Joan was always on the internet trying to self-diagnose her symptoms. The more she read about the range of medical issues that could contribute to how she was feeling, the more worried she became.

Finally, one evening Joan's sister went to visit her to share her concern. My friend knew that by isolating herself, Joan was exacerbating her fear. This time, Joan asked for help scheduling a doctor's visit. Joan also asked her sister to pick up some groceries at the local market because she had been too tired to stop on her way home from a very demanding job. When Joan saw her doctor, he recommended bloodwork and some additional tests. Joan really knew that ignoring her concerns was not the answer, so she mustered the courage to ask for and allow someone to help, realizing she didn't need to go through this experience alone. Joan's friends and family were there for support once she allowed herself to be open.

Have you ever experienced a medical issue that made you so fearful you didn't want to know what could be happening to your body? Or have you gone to the doctor but not been totally honest about your symptoms? When given a diagnosis, have you failed to ask for help in understanding it better?

In his book, *Power and Force: The Hidden Determinants of Human Behavior*, Dr. David Hawkins describes the emotional correlates of the energy fields, using a hierarchy of the Levels of Human Consciousness. The scale measures attitudes and emotions such as guilt, apathy, and fear to more positive emotions such as courage, willingness, love, peace, joy, and enlightenment. This information is important because in any given situation, we have a range of responses and emotions that can help us with a framework to become more conscious and aware of how to feel less separate and more in alignment with our Source.

Having a daily practice of asking the Universe, God, Divine Spirit, your Higher Power, Nature, or whatever your spiritual support is to guide and protect you, your family, and others every day, beyond any circumstances you or they may be facing, will help anchor you into a greater sense of faith, gratitude, peace, love, and trust.

WONDER WOMAN

How many of us are still wearing the "Wonder Woman" costume? Is it really a costume, or has it become part of the fabric of whom we have become? After listening to references to Wonder Woman in movies, cartoons, and comics, I became curious about this female superhero who appears to have it all together, is self-sufficient and confident, and doesn't need anyone.

During a conversation with my friend Bill, I asked him how he perceives the "having to do it all" woman. I always appreciate learning more from a male perspective. Bill said some of the women he had dated were very independent and determined and had a take-charge attitude. For him, this type of personality sometimes limited the opportunity to develop a truly open, collaborative, and giving relationship. Bill, laughing, stated he was a romantic at heart and loved women who appreciated the little things like him opening the car door, paying for dinner, and not feeling like everything had to be planned. He had recently broken off a relationship with a lovely woman with whom he had initially seen the possibility for a long-term committed relationship. She was self-reliant, determined, and very focused on her demanding career, while parenting her high school children and trying to balance a relatively new relationship. Although Bill and she enjoyed each other's company, traveling a distance to visit one another in different cities created another relationship barrier. Bill knew in his heart that their individual visions of what life would look like in two years were very different from each other, so they soon parted ways.

WAITING TO THE LAST MINUTE

One of my responsibilities in my leadership position was preparing and submitting grant proposals. One time I was working on a competitive grant that, if awarded, would provide a significant amount of funding to the school district to help improve students' health and wellness. The grant would enhance the physical education program, teaching students exercise and food choices for greater awareness of health and wellbeing. The 5:00 p.m. Friday deadline was only two days away, and I was procrastinating about sitting down to complete the final touches to the application with the needed data. I distracted myself by answering phone calls and emails rather than redirecting my energy to completing this important assignment. I knew I needed to focus, but anxiety about not getting it done correctly lurked in my mind. Finally, deciding to take the application home to work on it, which I had been doing each night that week, I packed it up in my briefcase.

By the time I got settled with my coffee and snack

at the dining room table, it was close to 9:00 p.m. Feeling tired and overwhelmed, I started judging myself for not planning very well. And I had not asked anyone to help me collect information. Why had I not reached out for help? Yes, everyone was busy, yet this was a priority they would have understood and been willing to help with. The application was much more complicated than I had anticipated. Rolling up my sleeves and pushing past my frustration with myself, I worked until early morning. Then it was done and I felt relieved. All I needed now was my secretary to type it up, and then I would deliver it to the post office by the deadline. The next day, my secretary was out sick, which was not in my plan. In that moment, I needed to see who might not have other deadline-driven assignments to help me get the grant completed. I truly needed to ask for help.

I recognized that I had been holding great stress, anger, and feelings of being overwhelmed in my body to accomplish this endeavor. My sleeping and eating patterns were just like those when I was in college preparing reports; this was a very old pattern of behavior that really was not serving me. What if I had set time on my calendar each day to do a part of the application? What if I had asked other people to help collect the information? What did it cost me in terms of my health, anxiety, and sleep to wait until the last minute? The upside of this story is that the application was hand-delivered with a 5:00 p.m.

postmark and the district was awarded the funds for the following school year. In addition, I had an opportunity to reassess how I could plan differently and ask for help.

THE LADDER

My amazing grandmother, Marion, loved her country home with its large vegetable and flower gardens. She loved to bake and always had a fresh pie cooling in the window. Her gardens reminded her of growing up in Maine. My grandfather had died a few years earlier, and she was still doing all the minor house repairs, painting, and tilling in the garden. One afternoon, Marion wanted to fix a few of the shingles that had lifted from the garage during the last windstorm. She knew she could ask my dad, but he was busy at work, and he had enough to do around his own house in the next town.

Deciding she would go slow and be careful, my grandmother got the ladder and leaned it against the garage. She climbed up and down, moving the ladder a few times, but the last time she didn't get it secured, so after she got back onto the roof, the ladder tipped and fell, leaving her on the roof. My grandmother stayed on the roof for a few hours until, out of the blue, a neighbor drove into the yard to see her on the roof! She found herself in this predicament because she always wanted to get things done in her timeframe. When she would ask for help, it might not always coincide with others' availability, so she did it herself. She was very grateful this time that someone happened to come by, and she promised us she would ask for help the next time.

Notice when you have an attitude of "I'll do it myself," when you know intuitively that seeking help and support will empower and bring satisfaction to you as well as others.

EXERCISE

Think of a time at work or at home when you felt someone else could help you out. What stopped you from asking?

_____

_____

_____

_____

_____

Do you believe you are responsible for training people not to help you? Are you willing to change your thoughts and behavior to ask for help? Identify a situation you would like to change.

_____

_____

_____

_____

_____

Where in your life do you procrastinate because you think you have to do something all by yourself or have not mapped out a plan?

_____

_____

_____

_____

_____

STRATEGIES: ASKING FOR HELP

- Call a friend, or accountability buddy for support when you find yourself swallowing your feelings and reaching for the food, cigarettes, alcohol, or some other habit of choice that no longer serves you.

- In the workplace, prioritize your activities. Seek support as needed. Design a plan of action.

- Be willing to ask for help.

- Discuss with family members what a healthy and happy home looks like. Mutually design a ten-minute family plan, such as identifying who is responsible for putting out the silverware, napkins, and drinks for dinner each night, and who feeds the dog and tidies the living room while you or a loved one prepare the meal.

- Ask more than one person to help you. Say "yes" when someone offers to help you.

SUMMARY

At times, we don't want to ask for help because we don't want to bother anyone. Fortunately, in my grandmother's case, it all worked out. When we listen to our intuitive self, our inner knowing, we usually know whether something is a good idea, dangerous, or we just need someone to listen or sit with us while we do something.

Some people will say they do not ask for help because it is selfish. You may find yourself feeling stuck in life, like a martyr, which reinforces that you have to do it all, when in reality, allowing someone to help you is as much for them as it is for you. Helping aligns with the invisible Law of Giving and Receiving. We deserve to be supported and loved in life. Are you willing to use your voice to ask for help?

Chapter 16

Being in Gratitude

"Develop an attitude of gratitude and give thanks
for everything that happens to you, knowing that
every step forward is a step to achieving something
bigger and better than your current situation."
— Brian Tracy

What would happen if you stopped long enough in your busy day to consciously take a deep breath and be grateful for your life? Are you willing to take that action right now?

Research shows that when people meditate or focus on being grateful for their family, friends, co-workers, and all the things in their lives, they are happier, more satisfied, less anxious, and more trusting that everything will work out. You may hear this referred to as living with an "attitude of gratitude."

More importantly, I ask you to take this moment to be grateful for your life! Many people have the ability to breathe unassisted, to walk without a cane or the use of a wheelchair, to have mobility in their hands and legs, to see the beauty all around them, to hear the alarm in the morning and the voice of a loved one, and so much more. Often, we take things for granted. The more gratitude we generate, the higher our vibration of life and love.

GRATITUDE JOURNAL

Writing in a gratitude journal is a habit I have nurtured for many years. However, it hasn't always been a consistent practice. Evenings before I went to bed on good days, I would write down three to five things that happened that I felt grateful for, or I would think of a few things and check them off in my head. Other days, I blew it off, maybe because I'd had a bad day, or felt lonely or depressed. Then it felt like one more thing to do, like make supper, get the report done, keep the appointments, exercise, drink more water, and eat healthily. I certainly knew how to beat myself up about all the things I should be doing, and this was one more on the list.

Then, I attended a workshop with a focus on changing habits. When I identified all the habits I knew were not serving me, it felt overwhelming. The presenter asked whether we would be willing to start a gratitude journal and stay committed to this practice for twenty-one days. It didn't have to be a fancy journal; a notebook would work. We could start with one of the habits we wanted to change like exercising, or becoming more patient and tracking our results. He shared that researchers Robert Emmons and Michael McCullough had asked groups of students to write down five gratitudes, five hassles, or five events that had happened over the past week for ten straight weeks. They found that the students who wrote down their gratitudes were happier and physically healthier.

As I committed to this practice, I reflected on the little gestures and significant things I was grateful for in my life. I noticed that writing down what I was grateful for and reading them later gave me a sense of satisfaction, joy, confidence, and fulfillment. I felt lighter and less absorbed with the day's irritations or drama. In fact, I found the activity relaxing. And yes, it was even fun to see what I might choose to be grateful for from the day. Instead of feeling impatient with the store clerk, I might give a warm smile and comment that it was a busy day for them. It made a difference to both of us. This practice made a significant shift in how I react to things; it has brought me greater peace in my heart and greater appreciation for others. Even my struggles and hardships have been softened by looking for some good in such situations.

THE VISIT

My client Linda shared with me her concern about an upcoming visit from Leah, her sister, who was flying into town for business. She described how Leah always acted overwhelmed, consumed with what wasn't working, or the drama in her life. Linda noticed she felt resentful toward Leah. Anytime they would talk, everything was always about Leah and rarely about what was going on in Linda's life. Linda loved her sister, so she coped with her behavior by saying yes and just listening rather than speaking up or presenting a different perspective.

For this visit, Leah had secured a hotel room, and she asked Linda whether she wanted to come to the hotel to stay and enjoy the amenities during their visit. Linda wanted to see her sister but remembered that her experiences with her were not always happy or enjoyable. In the past few months, Linda had been speaking her truth more and creating better boundaries with her children and friends, so she felt this would be a great opportunity to practice setting boundaries and creating an environment with Leah that was also conducive to meeting her needs and taking better care of herself.

Linda suggested they have dinner and invited her sister to stay overnight at her house the night before she was scheduled to check into the hotel. She also invited a friend over to share dinner with them.

During our conversations, Linda realized that as long as her perception of her sister and her responses were negative, she would get what she thought. She remembered what we often said in our sessions: "Where your attention goes, your energy flows."

After establishing some different supports for herself, Linda felt that releasing her old behavior of tolerating and resenting the visit allowed her to be more open and loving to her sister and to expend less energy trying to change her or her beliefs about her life. Linda was able to enjoy the visit and feel grateful to spend time with her sister, whom she really loved dearly.

My mentor always says, "Gratitude is the vibration that is harmonious with abundance." I am so grateful to have this profound teaching. When my focus is on my problems, struggling to make ends meet, or experiencing challenges in my work or personal life, I attract more of the same due to the level of my thoughts.

As I stopped dwelling on what I thought was missing in my life, I was able to start focusing on all the things I did have, such as family and friendships, love, a home, a car, pets, my health, money, and even the miracle of not having to think about how to take my next breath. When I shifted my energy and thoughts to focus on all the things I was grateful for, I felt a much greater feeling of appreciation and gratitude. Today, I am more mindful and

I have a conscious practice of gratitude. When I forget who I really am and choose to hop on that hamster wheel of worry and fretting, I stay in that mindset for less time and remember to give thanks to all the blessings in my life, no matter what.

MONEY

As a child, I was brought up with a belief that money aligned to happiness. You may have heard your parents say "Money doesn't grow on trees." You have to work hard and for long hours to take care of your family. We can all think of many more beliefs about money like this one that are not really true. This limited thinking, focusing on the lack or scarcity of money, keeps us stuck. We can listen to the news and read about several well-known people for whom money isn't an issue in achieving freedom and happiness, yet they were still unhappy. Money is never our True Source if we stay aligned to our spiritual beliefs. Yet we know that what we may love to do is often easier to acquire with greater financial abundance.

A few years ago, I was preparing for a ten-day trip to Prague, Vienna, and Budapest. I had a Travel Multicurrency Card I had purchased four years earlier that had not expired yet. One evening, I went online to check it. I had a problem signing in, could not remember my password, and after three tries, yes, got locked out. Did you ever notice that when we choose to do things late at night, we find out the offices are closed and we need to wait until the next morning?

About a week later, I remembered I had never followed up on the cash card. When I did, I was astonished to hear I had 500 Euros left on the card. Wow! I was super-grateful. It reinforced for me that our lives are abundant. The funds were always there; I had never tapped into them.

Alex, a client of mine, shared a story with me of finding in his desk a seventy-five-dollar cash rebate card for purchasing four snow tires earlier in the year. The expiration date on the card was thirty-five days earlier. Thinking it was too late, he started to throw it away when he noticed he was angry with himself for not paying attention or responding when first receiving the card.

He set his intention for a positive outcome and felt it was worth a try to inquire if he could still use the card. He called the dealer, explained he had just found the card, and asked what might be possible. After checking for him, the dealer came back on the line and told him there was a thirty-five-day grace period. This was day thirty-five! The dealer was sending him a new card for the same amount with a small reissue fee. Alex was so excited and grateful that he was open to believing things were possible. This event proved to him that by holding himself to a higher level of thinking and gratitude, greater abundance was possible.

EXERCISE

List five gratitudes you have for your family members, friends, or coworkers.

_____

_____

_____

_____

_____

Where at work or with your loved ones might you shift your perspective to feel more grateful, which will help boost your spirits?

_____

_____

_____

_____

_____

What is one area where you might be feeling negative or discouraged? What is one thing in this area that you are willing to be grateful about?

_____

_____

_____

_____

_____

STRATEGIES: MANIFESTING WITH GRATITUDE

- Maintain a daily practice of keeping a gratitude journal or notebook.

- Sit or lay quietly before you get up in the morning or go to sleep, spending a few moments to set the intention of the day or reflecting on the events of the day. Begin by saying "I am so happy and grateful that…."

- Acknowledge all the people you come into contact with by greeting them with a smile. Be in the vibration of appreciation and gratitude.

- Focus on your relationships, your home, all your resources both big and small, nature, and your health, wealth, and wisdom.

- Pay yourself first, no matter what the amount.

- Throughout your day, say "Thank you" to life.

SUMMARY

It is Universal Law that the higher our vibration of gratitude, the greater the level of abundance we have in our lives. I believe we are spiritual beings having a human experience. On many levels, we are more alike than we are different. We all have basic needs, and we have all made different choices that align with where we are today in our lives. Over the years, I have treasured those people in my life who are happy and have a spark of energy and light within them that is full of gratitude and love.

When we trust in God, Spirit, the Universe (or whichever word resonates for you with gratitude for all of our successes and failures), the flow of opportunities opens our hearts to feel more fulfillment and experience greater abundance. Our hearts also will open with greater capacity for love. Are you willing to open your heart?

Chapter 17

Trusting the Universe

"The moment you trust yourself,
you will know how to live."
— Johann Wolfgang von Goethe

We are all conditioned to the daily habits and circumstances of our lives. How many times have you heard someone say, "That's just who I am," "Life has dealt me a bad hand," or "Good things never happen for me"? Yes, that is how the outside world appears for some.

What if it could be different? What might that look like? How might a person act and think to reap a more profitable experience or mindset? Let's think about some of the world's great leaders who believed something was possible despite what all the surrounding people believed. Nelson Mandela spent twenty-six years in prison in the same country he later ruled as president. Victor Frankl, a Holocaust survivor, experienced that the only freedom he had was in his mind. Thomas Edison believed he could find a way to design circuitry for light versus using oil lamps. We all can think of someone who believed and trusted in themselves and their dream; their idea was possible when all circumstances said otherwise.

How many times have you waited for someone else to decide? How often have you doubted yourself or your idea and asked for people outside of yourself to confirm the answer? Did you spend time worrying about an outcome? Let me be the first to raise my hand to say "Yes"!

As I reflect on my habit of being afraid and worrying about things, it never changed what happened. Fear and worry are useless emotions, but they are seductive because they are familiar. We bring a lot of stress and strain into our relationships with ourselves and with others when we don't trust ourselves.

TRUSTING YOURSELF

Have you ever experienced that something just didn't feel right about a situation? But when asking if everything was okay, you were told it was "fine"? How many times have we not been honest with ourselves or with others, or had others not be honest with us? Do you become reluctant to act on that gnawing mental rehearsal of the question or action you know you should take, but you stop yourself?

We learn as children not to tell the truth about

how we are feeling. Children are sensitive to the words spoken to them, particularly by adults, teachers, parents, and community and church leaders. We did not want to get into trouble by telling the truth. We might have said we were staying after school when we really were going to a friend's house, knowing our parents had restricted any afterschool activities. As children, we may hear our parents say, "Don't tell your mother," or "Don't tell your father" because "They will be mad." Why are we surprised that trusting is not an easy attribute?

Some of us may have stories of feeling rejected or being abandoned. What I find amazing is how we have internalized the messages of our past to form the blueprint of how we live our lives. I am here to say we do have a choice, and we can still change and live a happier and freer life. But change requires us to believe in and trust ourselves. That takes time, practice, and support.

Who ever would have guessed that being an adult required a whole different level of learning and self-awareness? Trusting? It is freeing, courageous, and empowering. The more we act on what we feel and know to be for our highest good, the more the newer pathways of thought, trusting, and taking care of ourselves become automatic responses.

IT'S GOING TO BE ALL RIGHT

Growing up, I remember my dad always saying to me "It's going to be all right." I would worry about my mom, what others thought, my grades, my friends, and doing things right to feel loved. At the time, I felt my dad didn't understand my stresses, worries, or concerns. Consequently, I decided at an early age that what I had to say was not important, and it was safer to speak only when spoken to and to be nice.

Today, as I think about my father's words, I feel differently, and I have gained a healthier perspective. A dad, who did not verbally express himself well, found a way to acknowledge things were chaotic. He, too, would never say anything negative about anyone, yet he looked to comfort and encourage me to trust myself, let go of the things I could not control, and believe things would work out.

Recalling my own parenting, I often minimized my son's worries, making judgments as to what I felt real worries looked like. Although I believe I listened to him and showed compassion for his thoughts, I could have encouraged him to trust more in himself and in God, and not to let the outside world run his thoughts.

GREATER THAN YOU

My mom was a very religious woman with twelve years of parochial school education. She promoted a belief in a God who loved but also punished. I spent a lot of time in fear of what would happen if I did something really bad. Hence, I marched down the path of being a good girl, rarely questioning what appeared as reality.

I have been blessed with many experiences that have shaped who I am. These include physical and emotional abuse, shame, blame, and fears of uncertainty to transforming my beliefs and reframing my experiences for greater understanding and empowerment of myself and others. I deserve open-hearted, trusting, and loving relationships, and I feel at peace with myself and the decisions and dreams in my life still to come.

I believe we are all ever-evolving spiritual beings having a human experience. In saying that, I am sharing my authentic voice. You have the freedom to believe what is right for you. Consider that we are greater than our worries and our situations, and as I have mentioned earlier, most of us don't need to think about having to breathe. At some point, we all ask, "Who am I?" and "What is my purpose?"

Connecting to a Source greater than ourselves requires trust in something we can't see; it is a knowingness, a deep-seated belief, a feeling, and an energy that something is vibrating at a Higher Consciousness in our lives. We all have created and used different words that align with our beingness.

I have learned that when I get quiet and listen to my heart, a peace and calm washes over me. It can do the same for you. I worry less about having enough money, love, freedom, happiness, or peace because it is all about my connection with my Source.

BEING HONEST

How do you handle situations where someone you love is dishonest and denies the truth? When we are courageous and listen to and trust our own feelings, we ask questions from a loving heart.

Susan, a dear friend, shared with me her experience of being in a five-year relationship with Paul, a loving man who had remained friends with his ex-wife. Susan tried to understand and respect this long-established relationship, but she was never quite at ease with the idea. During the time they were together, she felt at times Paul relied on his ex's friendship. When she confronted Paul about this, Susan was honest about her discontent. Paul became defensive and said nothing was going on, so she shouldn't feel jealous or concerned. Feeling she might be overreacting, Susan acquiesced.

One weekend as Susan boarded a plane home from visiting her family, she received a text from Paul, who was planning to pick her up from the airport. However, the text was not designed for her but Paul's ex-wife and had been sent in error. It indicated that it had been good to see her when she stopped by at work. Susan's thoughts raced. She felt shocked, betrayed, and angry with him, as well as with herself, for not trusting and listening to her gut. This experience evolved into independent journeys for them both to listen, trust, and face their own needs and healing. Moving forward, no matter what happens, both of them will have a greater understanding of themselves. And that honesty provides greater empowerment and freedom.

EXERCISE

Think about a situation where you intuitively listened to your gut and felt something was off with a relationship at work or in your personal life. How did you address the situation that was bothering you?

_____

_____

_____

_____

_____

What old thought patterns of not trusting are no longer serving you?

_____

_____

_____

_____

_____

What do you fear will happen if you step into and trust your Divine guidance?

_____

_____

_____

_____

_____

STRATEGIES: TRUSTING THE UNIVERSE

- Create morning rituals that will help you set the day. Even 5-10 minutes of centering yourself will make a difference.

- Pray for daily guidance to serve the world in good faith.

- Know and trust that you do not need to have all the answers.

- At work, create a ritual. Focus on your priorities for the day. Review your calendar. Connect with the people you need to. A ritual like this will help set the foundation for being centered and focused for the entire day.

- Listen to your inner voice. Notice if you are feeling constricted thoughts, and take one small action step to shift the thought or response.

SUMMARY

We can all think of a time as children when we did not tell the truth because we did not want to endure the consequences. Adults may have labeled some of our stories as white lies. Sometimes, we got away with a lie or action. Believing in ourselves and trusting our own word is paramount to our peace and happiness. If we are not honest with ourselves, we gravitate to a world of fantasy, lack, and distraction. How often have you told yourself that tomorrow you are going to go to the gym, or stop eating so much sugar, or stop drinking? What happens when we start breaking our word to ourselves? We stop trusting what we say we want is important.

The good news is you have an inner knowing. You deserve and are worthy of greater happiness, love, peace, and joy. Trust you are not alone in this vast universe. Start today to believe in yourself, trust those hunches, and listen to the still small voice within you that your Divine Spirit is using to guide you every moment. Breathe.

Chapter 18

Believing in Your Dreams

"Don't be pushed by your problems;
be led by your dreams."
— Ralph Waldo Emerson

Nineteenth century American philosopher and author Ralph Waldo Emerson offers a code for living when he tells us to "be led by your dreams." Many of us learn and interact in life by seeing pictures in our minds. We imagine desired results. Once our mind has created an image, we can take action to make that image a reality.

GOAL VERSUS DREAM

One day, Ilene, a lifelong friend with whom I had shared the ups and downs of our lives' adventures, asked me to tell her more about the phrase I often use, "Believe in your dreams to live a life you love living." She was really asking for clarification about the difference between a goal and a dream.

Individually, we may all have different perceptions of what believing in our dreams and pursuing a goal may mean. For me, goals are the action steps to desired outcomes or dreams. I like the interpretation of goals and dreams given by the Perfect Leap Career and blog:

People often use the terms goal and dream as though they are one and the same. Goals and dreams should co-exist; however, they are not the same thing. If you only have dreams without goals to support them, it is easy to become overwhelmed with all the steps necessary to realize that dream. On the converse side, if you only have goals, but no dreams, you risk losing sight of your ultimate destination because you are so focused on the steps necessary to get there.

Brain research shows individuals who set intentions and focus their attention to achieve goals use one part of their brain. Clearly defining your goals can make the difference between success and just getting by. A dream is more aligned with a state of mind. It is energy and vision anchored in your mind from which you set goals to achieve. As my mentor says, "A dream without a plan is nothing but a wish."

BEING THE DREAM

As I was facilitating a group of open-hearted teachers, I reminded everyone that saying affirmations alone without a connection to the desired result usually will not lead to goals manifesting. To achieve a goal or dream, we have to understand what its achievement will look like. For example, what would it look like if I were the person who was healthier, wealthier, and happier? One needs to envision how that person will look, act, and feel. As another example, "I want more money" will not produce what one wants without clearly seeing oneself in the picture of their dream and feeling what that experience would be like. We have to believe through envisioning that a goal is achievable and then take action steps to make it happen.

During the group session, Micki stated that her aha moment was that without clarity or belief, her desired result was likely not attainable. She knew her dream was bigger than just wanting the "stuff" in life, and that she had a greater purpose and desire to make a difference with others. Micki realized that to have healthier relationships with family, friends, food, and money, she needed to take daily responsibility for her own choices and vision of how she looked and felt.

Two weeks later, Micki returned to the group and enthusiastically shared how she had shifted her perspective and willingness to be in action for a minimum of thirty days, eating mostly veggies, fruits, and protein, and committing to exercise at least three times per week. Taking charge of her thoughts, with her attention on the vision of being a healthier woman, provided her with greater freedom and happiness. Micki realized that by believing her dream was possible, changing her behavior, and being more mindful of her thoughts, she felt more alive, confident, and open to engaging in healthier relationships with not only herself but with her family, friends, and coworkers. Excitedly, Micki added that she was practicing daily gratitude. Her attitude and actions came to reflect her belief that something more was possible.

BELIEVING

We all have thought patterns and habits that keep our lives in motion. Our thoughts and beliefs have been hardwired in us. And, there is an infinite source of ideas in and around us if we are open to making them welcome in our mind.

As previously mentioned, for a few years I had the privilege of working with Mary Morrissey to become certified as a Life Mastery Consultant. Mary is a best-selling author, teacher, speaker, and coach. She is internationally known and supports thousands of individuals and groups across the globe in learning to transform their lives into ones they love with greater peace, happiness, and freedom. Mary encourages and teaches us to listen to the small voice within that whispers our deepest heartfelt desires and allows energy and enthusiasm into our hearts, anchoring them to a vision and desire of what we would love in our life. Then she guides us in taking small action steps to actualize that vision.

In August 1963, Dr. Martin Luther King, Jr.'s "I Have a Dream" speech was instrumental in shaping the minds of others with a shared vision and dream of what could be possible for this country. As Dr. King shared his deep inner beliefs and dreams, he spoke about the history of discrimination and his new vision for equality. His dreams did not reflect the country's past experiences, but while many could not see how his vision could be turned into reality, they shared his dream of freedom and equality for all. I found his speech compelling and resonated with his statement of a dream for his four children: "That they not be judged by the color of their skin but by the content of their character." Dreams can be compelling and life changing. We are all evolving and capable of making a difference for our families, community, state, country, and the world.

What is your dream?

OPEN TO POSSIBILITIES

Diane, a good friend, had owned her duplex home for about twelve years in a suburban community. For the last few years, she had found it more difficult to find reliable renters. She was tired and financially distressed about having enough to pay the monthly mortgage without the additional income. Feeling great angst because she did not want to sell her home, she decided it would be best to put her house on the market and get out from under the responsibility of being a landlord with all the unexpected expenses and home repairs it entailed.

Seeing no other option, Diane fixed up the other apartment after the last tenants moved out, and she went through the process and inconvenience of leaving her house several hours on the weekends and some evenings so the realtor could show it to interested buyers.

On two separate occasions, interested parties made offers, but ultimately, things fell through. Time was marching on and Diane did not have a buyer. Meanwhile, she had found new renters, but they were hesitant about continuing to rent, knowing that things might change with a new owner after their year's lease. When the second sale fell through, Diane called me to say she had decided to take the house off the market. She was discouraged and fearful that the money she had used to make repairs might now leave less for next month's mortgage.

Just as she felt her dreams slither away, out of the blue, Diane was contacted by an agency that provides apartments for disabled adults. The agency asked if the apartment was still available for a young man who would require around-the-clock care by the agency. Ironically, when Diane had first bought the duplex, she had been working for that same agency and had mentioned to her boss the availability of it as a rental property. However, at that time it was not on the bus line so not considered by the agency. Now Diane exclaimed with joy, "Here it is, twelve years later, and my dream has come true!" Diane was so happy that she could be making a difference in this person's life and that her prayers of not having to sell her house had been answered. Her duplex is now state-certified and inspected for individuals with disabilities. Because she had previously worked at the agency, Diane was also offered the opportunity to work weekends for the agency if she was interested in making additional income.

This story could not have been planned. The sequences of events were divinely guided. Diane's opportunities were far greater than her circumstances presented. She can now stay in a house she loves, and provide housing for this young man whose dad was losing time at work to stay home and care for his son. Plus, the son is in a wonderful apartment that has been accommodated to meet his special needs, and his father will not need to quit his job. Diane's last email to me said, "This situation is more than a rental check. It is about purpose and will always be God's miracle. I know I could not have done this alone.... The power of prayer and faith is magnificent!"

EXERCISE

When you allow yourself to think about some-
thing you would love, what thoughts come to
your mind?

_____

_____

_____

_____

_____

If you could wave a magic wand, and if money
and your circumstances were not an issue, what
would you love to be doing?

_____

_____

_____

_____

_____

When you attach yourself so personally to your
present circumstances, it limits your ability to
look at them in a different way. What are you
willing to do or say to provide a small opening
in the possibility of believing in your dream?

_____

_____

_____

_____

_____

STRATEGIES: BELIEVING IN YOUR DREAMS

- Reflect on what you would love to be, do, or have in life. Take one small step you can take today toward your vision.

- Love yourself as a unique Divine being. What would you need to tell yourself to change your mindset and to believe greater things are possible for you?

- Affirmation: *I believe in myself.*

SUMMARY

Our dreams are inspired by something inside us that is greater than we can figure out in that moment. If we could have, we would already have achieved our dream or known how to manifest it. Believing in our dreams when we think they are not possible requires faith, focus, purpose, and vision.

As children, when operating without judgment, we more freely allow ourselves to create, play, and design different scenarios of what our life might look like. My experiences up until now, both personally and professionally with other clients, have been about minimizing our desires and beliefs, thus giving more power to others' thoughts and beliefs as if they are true.

When you allow yourself to get quiet in your mind and heart, and you breathe into that space that is vast and all knowing, start asking yourself, "What would I love?"

Start believing in *you*.

Chapter 19

Being in Action

"If one advances confidently in the direction
of his dreams, and endeavors to live the life
which he has imagined, he will meet with success
unexpected in common hours."
— Henry David Thoreau

I have learned that being in action doesn't always look like having lots of things to do, the daily lists that we hold on to in our minds, on our phones, or on paper, written and placed on the desk. It starts with a willingness to let go of the distractions that pull us from our authentic self, to sit in the stillness, to anchor into and ask for guidance from a higher Source. Design your goals and actions based on being true to you.

My actions of helping others first kept me in action, making me feel like I was being productive. But in some ways, I was abandoning myself in the areas of self-care and relationships. Having the courage to take the next small action step to do what was going to lead me to what was for my highest good required me to be more present to the moment, listening to my intuition, and allowing my true Source to guide me for inner fulfillment and manifesting. That has now become my first step before I generate my list.

FOLLOWING YOUR PURPOSE

Reflecting on my purpose as a parent, family member, friend, teacher, school administrator, college instructor, consultant, and life coach, I have deeper questions regarding the influence we are having on our students in the education system. When I first started my career, I just wanted to make a difference in students' lives. And these thoughts were aligned to my values and teaching experiences. Initially, we teach the way we were taught, just as at times we parent based on our childhood experiences and beliefs. As we evolve in our understandings and are exposed to greater ways to perceive the world, we have greater influence on others.

Have you ever thought about how many students make choices based on someone else's dream for them? Are they being nice to please a family member, their peers, teachers, or a minister? Where is their voice in creating their own hopes and dreams? Do we encourage ourselves and others to think beyond circumstances to what could be possible? Many of us can remember as children imagining something bigger than our current level of comprehension. We enjoyed creating, wondering, and feeling courageous and free that something was possible. Then, as we have more lifetime experiences, we awaken to addressing a spiritual purpose.

IMAGINING MORE

Henry David Thoreau lived a simple life by his own design. Some of you may have heard his quote, "If one advances confidently in the direction of his dreams, and endeavors to live a life which he has imagined, he will meet with a success unexpected in common hours." Thoreau held a greater purpose through his imagination, and then he acted upon that purpose by deliberately choosing to go live simplistically at Walden Pond. Many of us acquiesce into living a life we know with less focus on purpose and focused intention.

Recently, I listened to an interview with Robert Kiyosaki, co-author with Sharon Lechter of *Rich Dad, Poor Dad*. While listening, I recalled my old perceptions about millionaires. I had read Kiyosaki's book a decade earlier, but with a belief that the good fortune he experienced happens to other people, but could not happen to me. Those who become millionaires know how to beat the system; they also had an earlier start and better supports.

This time, I heard Kiyosaki's message differently; my perception had changed in the years since I'd read his book. I realized that Kiyosaki, based on his experiences and teachings at an early age, had decided to live his life questioning the status quo and patterns of thinking regarding money. We all have that freedom. Kiyosaki chose to act and to learn as much as he could about a capitalistic society. He assessed the information he knew and used it to create a system to his benefit. He then spent years helping others repeat a similar system. During the interview, what struck me was his reference to purpose and being led spiritually. He did not negate that he was personally reaping significant financial abundance, yet he was also focused on helping others move out of a lack mentality. He explained how we are all required to act, to learn more, and to challenge our old beliefs if we are to succeed.

ACT OF RECEIVING

Acting is a mindset. For several decades, I have noticed many thought leaders living and speaking of leadership with purpose. Leaders are of service when they challenge our thinking so we achieve a greater mindset, awareness, and consciousness. In his book *Secrets of the Millionaire Mind*, T. Harv Eker talks about the Wealth Principle of blocking and receiving.

This principle shows up in all areas of our relationships and not just with money.

I love three practices that Eker suggests: being an excellent receiver, celebrating any level of receiving things, and pampering yourself—allowing yourself to give to yourself something good out of the ordinary, such as getting a massage, enjoying a weekend away, and so on.

Something I particularly resonated with as a receiver is how we often return a compliment with a compliment. This response seems to be particularly true for women. Someone says something nice about what we are wearing, but instead of receiving and responding with a loving thank you, we immediately feel compelled to respond with a return compliment. This deflection of energy does not allow the person to fully receive the gift the giver is giving. The more we are open to the mindset of giving and receiving, the quicker we will break down some of the blocks of abundance we have created in our thinking.

THE POWER OF NICE

I have learned that it doesn't matter how old you are; if your pattern for being nice is in your DNA, embrace it and be consciously aware of your intention in terms of how this pattern is serving you. While writing this book, I noticed I was vacillating in my own life between embracing the part of me that wanted to be nice and not hurt someone's feelings, which was my old stuff, and choosing to be kind and grateful and stay aligned to what was in my best interest.

During this time, my friend Nancy invited me and a few other women to go on vacation with her to St. Croix where she had a condo that could accommodate four people. Although I had another trip scheduled within a month of the proposed dates, Nancy was very accommodating and offered to change the dates so I could go. I immediately felt pulled to say yes because I had declined at least two other times for previous commitments and going as a group sounded like fun. I would have a room for a nominal fee for the entire week, so all I would need to do was look into points for airfare.

When the date to make a final commitment for the trip came around, I felt somewhat anxious, knowing I would be traveling to California two weeks after this proposed trip. Even though this vacation was a phenomenal opportunity, was I really acting responsibly based on my other traveling and financial commitments? Simultaneously, two of the other women had reassessed their family and financial obligations and regretfully declined the opportunity. In those moments, I really felt obligated not to let Nancy down. I even found another friend willing to share a room and expenses with me. I began to notice I was annoyed with myself for not sharing how I was feeling, and because Nancy had asked me before, I was trying to be nice to help her out. Wow! Isn't this interesting? Even while writing this book, being nice was still showing up while speaking my truth was being sidelined.

My next action was to do what I coach my own clients to do: Get quiet and ask for guidance about what it would be in my greatest good to do. Listening to my heart, I knew that what had contributed to me making my initial decision was I didn't want to say no again, thinking maybe then she wouldn't ask me again. And an old belief had come into my thoughts that once I said yes, I didn't want to bail. I had given my word. Yet I continued to notice it was creating more angst for me to try to make it all happen. Hmm. When we think we have control over making things happen and we don't listen to ourselves, that is a red flag to pay attention to. Gaining courage and knowing what I needed to do, I went back and was honest with Nancy. Graciously, Nancy understood why I had changed my decision, and I felt good being honest and true to myself as well as her.

SATISFACTION

Have you ever looked at the word "satisfaction"? The last six letters in the word spell "action." I point this out often with my coaching clients and in workshops as people share their stories about feeling stuck in a job, or about the issues they have with co-workers, family members, and friends that result in them not taking care of themselves. To have satisfaction, you must take planned action.

Colleen is a good friend and colleague whom I have watched and admired for a number of years as she transformed the quality of her health and wellness. She has released more than forty pounds. I watched her identify a positive mindset and dream of how she wanted to feel and look. She accessed opportunities to design food plans and to track her food and exercise. Colleen also surrounded herself with like-minded people who enjoy feeling good about themselves, and she has enjoyed their support. Her confidence and energy have soared. Things that used to feel laborious to her now feel effortless. And she is in action when it comes to making choices that will serve her being healthy. She has truly inspired me.

EXERCISE

What is one action you can take in the next five minutes to keep you moving toward a desired goal?

_____

_____

_____

_____

_____

What sustained action are you willing to commit to that will get you closer to a desired result, such as better health and wellness for yourself? What is stopping you?

_____

_____

_____

_____

_____

Spend a few moments in silence. Drop into your heart space and ask, "What action is for my highest good?" Write it below.

_____

_____

_____

_____

_____

STRATEGIES: BEING IN ACTION

- Make a list of your big projects. Under each item, brainstorm a list of actions needed to complete each project.

- Identify one very small action you could do in the next 5-10 minutes to move you forward in achieving a goal.

- Identify a start date and a completion date on your calendar for projects.

- On your calendar, schedule regular exercise and personal commitments to support your health and wellness.

- Honor your commitments with yourself. Seek an accountability buddy.

- Ask yourself, "What if I could?" when you feel stuck in doubt.

SUMMARY

Being in action does not always equal movement. Sometimes, when we choose not to respond, we have decided not to act in that moment. Pausing is an important strategy that allows us to go inside ourselves and ask what is the truth behind our reason for acting. Even firefighters spend a great deal of time planning, preparing, and evaluating what is required before they act so they can be of ultimate service to others.

Living much of my life as a multi-tasker, I have had to learn to step back, be more focused with intention, and take a deep breath. Often, we get so busy with so many plates spinning in our minds that we tend to take shallow breaths and never get grounded concerning what is really needing the most attention. When you take this moment and ask your true Source for guidance beyond your own thinking, more freedom is available along with more expansive thought. Taking one action step will move you toward your desired result and dream. Trust in yourself and seek support. You do not have to do it alone.

Chapter 20

Dancing with the Winds of Change

"The secret of change is to focus all of your energy not on fighting the old, but on building the new."
— Socrates

Living in the Northeast prompts me to awaken my awareness of the seasons. More importantly, I am so happy and grateful for the changes in my life and my spiritual connection with my soul and who I am. They align with how spring brings new beginnings, as the lime green color of fresh grass and tiny buds and leaves emerge on the trees. Yellow daffodils look like trumpets singing with a sound of color against the earth. Life is optically coming alive, and so are you.

Summer offers memories of lighthearted moments at the beach as the sand filters through my toes, feeling the sun shining on my face, and hearing the shrill voices of children as they splash against the waves.

Autumn is my favorite season because it offers

spectacular vibrant colors of red, orange, and yellow hues on the leaves of trees, an amazing visual representation of nature's cycle of change. The beginning of winter offers a time of reflection. The trees stand as silhouettes of solitude, already in hibernation, with snow anchored to their branches, as they deeply prepare for the regeneration of another season in the cycle of life. We get to choose how much we engage in the dynamics of our lives.

We are all part of this Universe, the natural rhythms of life. And are we really paying attention and living with deep connection to our mind, body, and spirit?

PAYING ATTENTION

Nature offers us so many lessons. Spending time outdoors can bring a whole different feeling and change of attitude. Making conscious choices helps me to change perspective for greater healing and peace. What I appreciated and loved about my grandmother was her passion for the outdoors. She delighted in digging in and rototilling the earth, planting seeds, and watching things grow. She taught me to get quiet, close my eyes, and listen to the wind blow against the blades of grass and rustle the leaves on the trees. To this day when I go outside, I get the sense of peace and centering when I allow myself to just *be*.

Are you paying attention to things in your life with a sense of peace and calm? If your answer is "No," what if you could? Are you willing to start giving yourself at least five to seven minutes a day to get quiet, feel your feet on the ground, and know all you have to do in that moment is breathe? What if I were to tell you that if you did this daily, it would change your life?

Babies, children, teenagers, and adults of all ages experience life's transitions. School, work, vocations, relationships at home and at work, our health and wellness, time, and money freedom are forever changing. When I was thirty, I read Jenny Joseph's poem "When I Am Old" about how when the speaker is old, she will wear purple and do many other fun things she couldn't do earlier in her life. I remember thinking, "Why not now?" Basically, how we engage in the dance of life is all about choice and mindset.

ADJUSTING THE SAILS

One afternoon, my son stopped by for a visit. He listened to my story of trying to coordinate with a few colleagues to meet a deadline and complete a job. I had delegated some of the work and was worried about it getting finished on time. He reminded me of a quote: "You can't direct the wind, but you can always adjust the sails." Before he left that day,

The Art of Being Nice

he wrote the quote down on a piece of paper and placed it on my refrigerator to remind me. When I see it, it makes me smile because I see his wisdom shared and reflected back to me. It is amazing the things we think we have control over and really don't. Yet we spend a lot of our waking hours worried and trying to fix, change, or replay the past in our minds. No wonder we get tired! How many times have you had to adjust your sails?

When I was a very little girl, my grandmother made me a beautiful turquoise dance dress with a material that shimmered when I twirled. I felt like a ballerina. I never worried about my dance steps. Although very shy, I couldn't wait to get on stage, feeling free and sensing so much joy and fun. Over the years, we learn from very well-intentioned people like our teachers, parents, ministers, family members, and friends that we need to do things perfectly or correctly, and often, the feeling of joy and spontaneity in our hearts deflates like a helium balloon. If we let it!

HOLDING ON

Like all of us, years of experience have gifted us with maturity, wisdom, grace, love, heartbreak, hurt, anger, disappointment, acceptance, forgiveness, and so much more. For many years, I found myself going along with others because I was more afraid of the unknown or of stepping into my own truth and voice. It was time for me to let go of the old patterns, not take myself so seriously, and just go for it.

My friend Rose always liked to have a plan and know where, when, and how everything was going to happen. Keeping things status quo was comforting to her. During a conversation over coffee one morning, she told me she had been going to a business networking group. One individual there was a financial advisor who extended an offer to her for a complimentary review of her portfolio. Rose immediately responded that she already had an advisor and let the thought go. However, after a few months, Rose reconsidered the opportunity.

After sharing her story, Rose asked me whether she should change financial advisors. Having made a few of my own financial blunders over the years, I asked her what kind of relationship she had with her current planner and whether she felt good about it? I sensed her hesitation and could hear in her voice that she didn't have the same feeling of being informed, although indicating they did meet annually. I heard her justifying that she was a loyal client, and while she thought she might like to explore another provider, she had been working with this individual for more than a decade and he had supported her through some difficult financial times. During our conversation, I asked Rose if she stayed in other situations in her life to be nice, loyal, or caring, or because she felt obligated.

Taking a piece of paper out of my purse, Rose and I made a T-chart of the pluses and minuses of her current advisor and company. Through this exercise, Rose became aware that she stayed in situations because once she made the initial decision, she felt it was final. Rarely did Rose allow herself to reconsider or change her mind based on more current information.

To make a more informed decision, Rose decided to set up an appointment to learn more. A few weeks later, Rose called me to say she was very happy she had learned more; she had received more strategies in one session than she felt she had for a number of years. Reflecting on the experience, Rose noticed her desire not to change was more out of being loyal and comfortable and not knowing what else was available.

This appointment had helped her to make a decision to change advisors and put a voice to her financial needs in a more confident way.

Maybe you can identify with this limiting belief, "The devil you know is better than the devil you don't." Where in the world did we learn that? Not to mention the use of the word devil? Why would we want to engage with anything that held that vibration of energy for us? Today, I encourage you to ask more questions and speak up. Know that you get to take care of yourself and you don't have to resist change just to be nice.

DANCING WITH THE MEMORIES

Losing a family member or friend brings not only feelings of sadness for the individual but also thoughts of previous losses in your own life. This change is a universal one.

I once attended a beautiful memorial for a kind friend, Jeff, who passed unexpectedly. As I sat in the church and listened to "Amazing Grace" being sung, my thoughts drifted and danced to the others who had profoundly touched my life and were no longer on this earth.

A heartfelt selected slideshow displayed Jeff's nature photography, which was the most beautiful I have ever seen. Jeff lived life to the fullest. He loved life, took risks, was compassionate, and had a contagious laugh. Jeff was a handyman who worked on his own schedule and was always willing to help others. He was always offering to power-wash my deck or fix my plumbing, windows, doors, and so much more. Jeff was a special man who touched many hearts and made you feel special. Particularly at times like these, you reflect on how quickly things can change.

TIMES ARE CHANGING

Is life going faster? One universal truth is we all have twenty-four hours in a day. How we use that time varies as much as the number of people on this planet. I have reflected on this truth differently in recent years. I ask myself: How am I using my time? Can I read the newspaper versus sitting listening to the same headlines repeatedly on the television? Why am I procrastinating finishing this book? Am I directing my attention to what I truly say I want? Or am I letting all of life's opportunities keep me busy and distracted?

Technology has supercharged our communication and connectivity. I am not sure I believe relationships and intimate human interactions have been positively enhanced by social media and other forms of technology. Vidya Frazier, author of *Awakening to the Fifth Dimension: A Guide for Navigating the Global Shift*, suggests we are moving from the third dimension to the fifth dimension, where there is greater acceptance, love, and collaboration for the world. Thousands of researchers and leaders are speaking about this issue of global consciousness.

Collective consciousness has been known to change the level of vibrational energy when we focus and place our attention on our intentions. For example, for several years, the Global Peace Project affiliated with State University of New York at Albany focused on seeking participants in a collective consciousness during the month of January to reduce the number of crimes reported in the City of Albany. During these focused time periods, a reduction of incidences and crimes were reported. This data was used to support ongoing research. If this can happen when group consciousness is focused for good and peace, what can your life look like if you took on these principles and applied them to your own life for your highest good? As we change and become more conscious in thoughts and actions, we have a direct impact and responsibility on the world changing.

EXERCISE

As you look at making changes in your life, what is one thing you can do to make a change go more easily?

_____

_____

_____

_____

_____

Do you find yourself forcing things to just get them done, even in situations that you do not have control over? How will changing your perception of the situation impact the outcome?

_____

_____

_____

_____

_____

If you could change one area in your life, what would it be and what action would you take?

_____

_____

_____

_____

_____

STRATEGIES:
DANCING WITH THE WIND OF CHANGE

- Consciously change your mindset and language (internal and external) from a pattern of "I don't or I can't" to "What if I could?" This simple language change will alter your thinking and open you to possibilities.

- Imagine your desired result. Place yourself in the picture you have envisioned and feel how it feels several times a day. Do not try to make it happen. Allow the day's events to guide your actions. By not knowing the "how," many unexpected, "out of the blue" occurrences are more likely to happen.

- Affirmation: *It is a joy for me to express myself. I trust I am Divinely guided.*

SUMMARY

We are all dancing with the winds of change. As Bob Proctor, a well-known professional business coach and trainer of multi-million-dollar organizations, says about working with change, "The one thing we are guaranteed is change, but personal growth is a choice."

A mantra I often say is "All things happen for a reason." I am often amazed when events happen "out of the blue" that cannot be explained. Someone reading this book may believe that the things that happen in life are just coincidences. Others know that circumstances can be changed by our personal thoughts, perceptions, and actions in a much greater way as we become more aware of our thoughts and feelings about them.

As nature repeatedly shows us, we cannot control the forces of nature. Being open to change with less resistance offers an easier flow. Sometimes when we are walking on uneven ground, we may need to be more deliberate in taking our steps and more aware of our intentions. Other times when we are walking in life but not paying attention, we are surprised when things happen; we may then try to brace ourselves from the unexpected fall to the ground, possibly bruising or even breaking a bone in the process. Trusting that Spirit is always with us helps us interact and embrace life more easily and effortlessly—just like dancing in the wind.

A Final Note

The Art of Being Nice

This book is written with women and men, sisters and brothers, mothers and fathers, daughters and sons, coworkers, and friends in mind who demonstrate life patterns of compromising their truths, limiting their God-given talents and abilities, and limiting the power of using their voices. It provides an opportunity to reflect, identify behaviors that no longer serve them, and receive support in leading a life of greater freedom, happiness, and love.

Writing this book has offered me an amazing journey of self-discovery, healing, and transformation. I want that for you as well. What has being nice and keeping quiet cost you? Do you hold resentments, and do you not dare to say what is really in your heart and mind? Are you afraid to lose love and attention? Might you lose your job? Will your speaking up in your family make waves?

I guarantee that changing how you think about and approach life will open you up to greater confidence, satisfaction, and love—the love of yourself.

As I mentioned in the introduction, the song "Amazing Grace" comes to my mind. I was truly lost, and I was hardly aware of it! I was trying so hard to be the good girl, staying in control and pleasing others to get attention and love from them and to make others happy. I was compromising my own happiness, freedom, worthiness, and self-love. I am pleased to say I have been able to let go of the grip that many of the stories had on me even into adulthood. The good news is you, too, can shift and transform your personal story of struggle, betrayal, isolation, and minimizing your worth and love.

In this book, you have learned from others' stories and through self-reflection questions and specific coaching strategies. I hope you have and will continue to apply them to yourself to strengthen how you love yourself in a healthy way.

As you apply the wisdom, knowledge, experience, strategies, and techniques offered in this book, you will achieve what this book's subtitle promises: the power to own your voice for greater freedom and fulfillment!

Now what? Now that you have read and finished this book, what actions are you willing to take to experience greater happiness and freedom? What dreams and goals are you going to set? What resources, support, or coaching might you seek?

I challenge you to act now! Knowledge is not power; applied knowledge is power. You can read or listen to all the relationship-building, diet, exercise, and self-improvement books and media in this world, but unless you choose to apply a change of thought and perceptions, you will only minimize your successes and the heartfelt freedom you want for yourself and others.

In the exercise lines below, list ten action steps with a "by when" date you will commit to taking them within the next ninety days as a result of reading this book.

1._____
2._____
3._____
4._____
5._____
6._____
7._____
8._____
9._____
10._____

Now summarize what this book has meant for you. For example: By reading this book, I am so happy and grateful that I gained greater insight and strategies to feel more confident and empowered by my actions. This is important to me because....

_____
_____
_____
_____

Thank you for taking time to read my book. I invite and encourage you to contact me with feedback. Please share with me what you liked and what you disliked so I can improve it for the next printing.

More importantly, tell me about you, your challenges, and your obstacles and adversities so I can help you. In fact, I would like to offer you a complimentary, no-obligation 30-60-minute consultation by phone, Skype, Zoom, or in person (if geography allows) to see how I can help and assist you. Visit my website at: ALeaderInYou.com or email me: diane@ aleaderinyou.com.

With gratitude and love, I wish you happiness, freedom, and abundance as you live a life you love!

Diane Albano

How to Auto-Correct the Three Most Important Relationships in Your Life: Family –Work –Friends

"If you can't say anything nice,
don't say anything at all."
— Mom

I was raised on this mantra. Perhaps you were as well.

In fact, my upbringing valued this approach above all else. It was ingrained in me that if I was simply "nice," rewards and recognition would naturally follow.

This belief was so hardwired in my mind and soul that I carried it as a "fact" with me into adulthood, totally trusting that I was well-equipped for whatever might lie ahead.

Always passionate about working with people, I became a teacher, school administrator, and college instructor.

Following my divorce, I became a single parent, raising a son.

Holding firm to the belief of being nice, I tried to balance home and work responsibilities with a smile on my face while still saying yes to every new work project, deadline, and opportunity. This behavior generated considerable guilt because it caused me to miss many of my son's games, school presentations, and field trips.

I found the whole balancing act a huge struggle. Still, I kept a smile plastered on my face in public, while in private I was defeated, discouraged, and disheartened.

Over these years, my job was my primary identity. As I became more and more attached to my work life, and tried to get my sense of meaning and fulfillment through my work, things began to deteriorate. I knew I wasn't giving my son or myself the attention and care we both required, but I was unaware of any other path.

At a gut level, I knew this situation couldn't last forever. Yet I still desperately clung to "being nice" and accommodating as my highest values. What I didn't know was that in the process, I was slowly strangling my soul.

A pivotal moment for me occurred in 2015 after the death of my father.

A month later, I started dating a man who was very much like my father in personality and temperament. I believed he was heaven sent. He was loving, kind, and caring. We even booked a marvelous trip to Hawaii several months in advance.

Unbeknownst to me, my relationship with this man was a part of my grieving process. As time went on, something just wasn't "in-sync" between us. We had different interests and desires, and I had to admit to myself that I wasn't being honest with him or with me by continuing the relationship.

Two weeks prior to the trip, things came to a crossroads for me. I realized I wasn't being nice to him by failing to share my feelings.

So, I took a deep breath, and I told him I couldn't go on the trip with him. It was an excruciatingly difficult conversation, but absolutely necessary. I knew I wasn't being fair to myself or to him. As a result, I made the trip by myself.

My biggest lesson in this situation was to be true to myself and others by speaking my truth.

I could see that many of my coaching clients, both female and male, had also lost using their true voice.

And so, I folded this critical piece into my coaching groups: How to authentically manage the three most critical relationships in our lives by giving a voice to what we're historically trained to hold back. Below we'll look at each of these relationships.

FAMILY RELATIONSHIPS

Other than our relationship with ourselves, family is undoubtedly the most important relationship we have.

Yet we often tend to put the least effort into nurturing and cultivating family relationships. We seem to think these relationships should come naturally. After all, they're family!

But family relationships can be the most fragile of all. We'll hold in our anger at coworkers, only to let it spill out at home onto our unsuspecting family.

We won't tell a friend she's disappointed us one time too many, but we sure will complain about her to our spouse, significant other, mom, or adult child.

We'll scream at our kids to clean up their dishes in a voice and tone we wouldn't dream of using with our boss.

For many of us, family is where we tend to dump all our emotions. It's a soft place to fall. A place to let it all hang out.

But in the process, we can do some serious damage to our family relationships.

And, of course, in our work-crazed society, we tend to shortchange family to the benefit of career responsibilities.

I know I certainly did.

Take a moment right now to identify what you consider are the most important areas of your family relationships.

What would you love to be doing with your family to build better relationships?

How can you possibly enhance your connection with your spouse, children, parents, and siblings?

Brainstorm what would help you feel better. What might be one step you can take?

"Your time is limited so don't waste it living someone else's life. Don't let the noise of others' opinions drown out your own inner voice."
— Steve Jobs

Let me jump-start the process with some ideas:

- If you can't get to your daughter's soccer game, ask someone to **record a video** and then watch it with her later, while she fills you in on the back-story of every play.

- Slip a little **note of encouragement** into your son's lunch or backpack before he leaves for the day.

- Spend **sixty minutes on the weekend** pre-planning the coming week's meals.

- **Get your family to help.** How can everyone pitch in and help the family unit run more smoothly? We often expect people to know we're tired and that we need them to step up and share some responsibilities. But they don't. We have to teach them. Come up with a five-minute family plan such as: 1) Everyone is going to pick up two pieces of dirty clothing and place them in the laundry basket, or 2) The younger child is responsible for putting out the silverware, napkins, and drinks for dinner each night, while the older child feeds the dog and tidies the living room while I prepare the meal. Teach your family how to participate.

- Consciously **change your language** (internal and external) from a pattern of "I don't" or "I can't" to "How can I? How do I?"

This simple language change will alter your thinking and open you up to possibilities. And your family will experience the shift as well.

Notice that all these action steps are small and doable. Start with these manageable steps and you'll begin to see big improvements in your family relationships.

WORK RELATIONSHIPS

Grab a pen and paper and jot down what it is about your work that you just love. What lights you up about it? What brings you joy and gets you up in the morning?

Rest in those thoughts for a few moments. Recall what it is about this work that drew you to it.

Now, what are your work challenges? What concerns do you face daily?

Quite often, those challenges involve relationships with people in your workplace.

Whether you own a business, hold a leadership role within a department, are part of a team, or work at home, the success of your work relationships determines the bulk of your happiness and your career accomplishments.

To get back to focusing on what lights you up about your job, you need to have effective personal relationship skills.

Brainstorm some quick ideas about how you can spend more of your time doing those things that light you up, and less of your time involved in conflict, feeling overwhelmed, and in frustration.

If your brain is telling you "Nope! Not a thing I can do!" or "I've tried and those people are hopeless. We're stuck!", take a few deep breaths and ask your heart for the answers.

Your heart does have the answers. You just don't know it yet.

"The best and most beautiful things in the world cannot be seen or even touched—they must be felt with the heart."
— Helen Keller

Use these ideas to nudge your heart into giving you the answers:

- How can your **calendar** help? Schedule an appointment with yourself. Set reminders on your phone that are daily affirmations for when your work slump usually hits.

- If a supervisor, where can you **delegate** some work? (Before your brain says "No!", ponder this thought a little more.)

- If you are feeling overwhelmed, will you **ask for help**?

- Schedule a **fifteen-minute walk** outside each day to get your creative juices flowing again.

- Periodically **invite colleagues** to join you on your walk so you can build your relationship and rejuvenate their creativity as well.

- Create a **morning ritual**. Arrive, get settled, focus on your priorities for the day, review your calendar, and speak with your secretary if you have one. A ritual like this will help set the foundation for an entire day of being centered and focused.

- **Avoid reading or responding to email** for the first twenty minutes of every day.

- Determine the **top two things you'll focus on each day**. Do some of those big things first, and the little things will come more easily and swiftly. And some of them will disappear entirely!

Distractions and unfocused thinking are two of the worst destroyers of effective work habits and accomplishments.

Why does it feel so good to sacrifice important tasks and projects for trivial and easy tasks? Because every time we respond to an email, sharpen pencils, get a cup of coffee, read an online article that caught our eye, or chat with a coworker, we get a tiny hit of the drug called "fake accomplishment." And it feels good to "accomplish" things.

But all those tiny fake accomplishments are akin to a good hit of sugar. A candy bar, or a cupcake feels oh so good in the moment, but too much and you feel ill, lethargic, and useless.

Start thinking of those unimportant tasks as pure white refined sugar: unhealthy, addictive, and a time stealer.

Keep your thoughts and your vision on your two important tasks each day. Thoughts and visions are powerful anchor points for men and women. Use them to your advantage.

At the end of your workday, congratulate yourself on what you did accomplish that makes a difference in your career and in your contribution.

FRIEND RELATIONSHIPS

Are you tempted to skip this section about social relationships? About friends?

If so, that's not surprising.

The working person may not have time for friends, considering them a luxury they can't afford.

Some people are in isolation, overwhelmed and lonely, and not knowing how to go out and create friendships.

It's critical that we enrich our lives with people outside of our family because they bring a different perspective and different dynamic—a different energy—than what we experience all day at work or at home.

Friends complement our lives and bring balance by adding a dose of fun and play. When we don't get enough fun or play, we become heavy in thought, and even further isolated and overwhelmed.

Anyone who has ever been on a sports team understands the meaning of team. And relationships. And how important they are. They get that.

But some people never had that team experience, and as adults, they may not be sure how to cultivate friendships.

Here are some ideas for building friendships and expanding your world of support:

- **Find Your Tribe:** Think about what you would love to do. If you love books, find a dynamic book club and join. If you're a cyclist, join a local cycling team that will challenge you physically and build friendships.

- **Volunteer:** Volunteering is good for you, good for the community, and great for finding new friends.

- **Reconnect with Old Friends:** Reconnecting with old friends—in person or on social media—is a great way to strengthen old relationships and discover new friends.

- **Think Consistency:** If you find it hard to commit to friendships, then join a club, group, or organization that meets regularly. This gives you a natural and consistent starting point for building friendships with like-minded people.

- **Be Vulnerable:** Listen to your inner voice and know what is best for you. Share the vulnerable side of yourself and your friendships will deepen beyond the superficial.

Friendships are important—for your health, happiness, and success. Add these relationships to your life and you'll experience a greater sense of fulfillment and contribution.

WHAT'S NEXT?

These three key relationship groups—family, work, and friends—can be a source of tremendous happiness and satisfaction for you. In many cases, all that's needed are a few tweaks to experience enormous positive shifts.

And these tweaks are something you can do. You are greater than your circumstances.

If you still feel that you're off-balance—that your life is off-course in one or more of these areas—I recommend talking with someone who has been through it and who can help lead you through it as well. Because none of us can see our own stuff.

Let me be that person for you.

I invite you to schedule a time with me so I can offer you guidance and support on the steps to feeling a greater sense of aliveness, more passion, and more time for the relationships and things that are most important to you.

Are you ready? Let's get started!

Schedule your time with me at:
Diane@ALeaderInYou.com

About the Author

Dr. Diane Albano is a talented, well-known, and highly skilled, certified professional leadership consultant and life coach. Her experience as a parent, teacher, administrator, speaker, and coach helps Diane connect with and support individuals and teams to identify the most important issues they are facing and gain greater success and fulfillment. As an educational leader serving in public school systems for more than forty years, Diane has worked with teachers and administrators across the country to provide leadership strategies with a focus on instruction, special education, and supports for school improvement. During the mid-2000s, she was an adjunct instructor at Sage Colleges and the State University at Plattsburgh of New York with a focus on educational psychology and educational leadership.

Now retired as a college instructor and school administrator, Diane continues to provide educational leadership consultation and coaching to schools engaged in school improvement training to support greater performance and results for teachers and students. Diane also continues to serve as an executive coach for participants in the Sage Doctoral Program for Educational Leaders in Albany, New York.

Diane focuses her heartfelt passion, energy, unique knowledge, and training to support and empower her leadership and life coaching clients in creating results so they can live lives they will love with greater freedom and fulfillment in their health and wellness, relationships, careers, and finances. She is the founder of LEAD Consulting and Coaching in Delmar, New York. As a certified professional life coach, Diane offers individual and small group VIP Programs for women and men who are committed to having transformational results in their personal or professional relationships. Additionally, Diane is available for speaking engagements.

Contact Diane at:
Diane@aleaderinyou
ALeaderInYou.com

About Leadership and Life Coaching

If you want to *be a leader in your own life*, stand confidently in your professional and personal life, and experience greater fulfillment, taking action is your best option!

You may have arrived at the point where you are aware that you want more happiness, freedom, and fulfillment in life. Or you may want a different result in your career. Either way, a change is required, and change can be daunting, scary, and exciting.

Whatever your goals, Leadership and Life Coach Diane Albano can help you clarify and identify the gap between where you are and what you most desire. The transformative work you will do will not only make your life more abundant, but it will equip you to better support those who rely on you at work or at home.

The hardest part is making the decision to say "yes" to you. If you are willing to change some of those habits and patterns of behavior that no longer serve you to create personal goals and a vision for your health and wellness, career, relationships, financial freedom, and time, then it's time to say "yes" to you.

It's that simple.

If not now, when?

To discover how Diane can help you, visit her website and sign up for a no-obligation 30-60-minute coaching consultation by phone, in person, or Zoom.

www.ALeaderInYou.com

Book Diane to Speak at your Next Event

When it comes to choosing a professional speaker for your next event, you will find no one more talented and supportive—no one who will leave your audience or colleagues with greater insight or a change in perspective for themselves and others—than Diane Albano. Whether your audience is small or can fill a convention hall, whether it is in North America or abroad, Diane can deliver a customized message of inspiration for your meeting or conference.

Diane understands your audience does not want to be "taught" anything, but is rather interested in hearing stories of inspiration, achievement, and real-life people becoming more empowered to use their voices to create lives they will love. Diane's speaking approach is to share genuine, heartfelt stories using humor and gratitude. Her passion and inspiration have been proven to help people achieve extraordinary results.

Diane is available for speaking engagements at civic organizations, women's groups, leadership seminars, educator conferences, parent groups, and to any organization she can benefit. Topics include but are not limited to:

- Coaching and Mentoring in the Workplace

- Leading Change with Others

- Essential Elements for School Turn Around

- 3 Keys to Manifesting Abundance

- Change Your Thoughts, Change Your Life

- Creating Greater Freedom and Fulfillment in Your Life

- The Power and Pitfalls of Being Nice

If you are looking for a memorable speaker to leave your audience wanting more, book Diane Albano today! To find out if she is available for your next meeting, visit her at:

www.TheArtofBeingNice.com
www.ALeaderinYou.com
Diane@aleaderinyou.com
518-362-7702